On This Day In

KINGSPORT HISTORY

On This Day In

KINGSPORT HISTORY

BRIANNE WRIGHT

THE History PRESS

Published by The History Press
Charleston, SC
www.historypress.net

Front cover, clockwise from top left: Douglass High School basketball team, 1949. *Archives of the City of Kingsport*; Rotherwood Mansion postcard, undated. *Archives of the City of Kingsport*; Kingsport Grocery Company fire. *Archives of the City of Kingsport*; Carolina, Clinchfield and Ohio Railway Passenger Station postcard, undated. *Archives of the City of Kingsport*; Soapbox derby. *Archives of the City of Kingsport*; Kingsport High School baseball team, undated. *Archives of the City of Kingsport*; Kingsport Press Strike. *Archives of the City of Kingsport*; Parade float in Independence Day Parade, 1955. *Archives of the City of Kingsport.*

Back cover, top: Kingsport Utilities Fair Booth, 1949. *Archives of the City of Kingsport.*

First published 2016

Manufactured in the United States

ISBN 978.1.46713.762.1

Library of Congress Control Number: 2016948316

CONTENTS

ACKNOWLEDGEMENTS

Putting this book together has been an interesting, demanding (but fun) process. I definitely could not have done it alone.

First and foremost, thank you to all who have supported and donated to the Archives of the City of Kingsport. Your contributions have been invaluable to preserving Kingsport's history, and they have allowed me to share that history with the community.

To the Friends of the Archives Board: Sharon Brown, George Hutchins, Andrae and Jessica Robinson, Becca Wright, Jim Wright, Toni Cave, Ginny Snow, Gail Campbell, George Hutchins, Jane Scott, Kenny Stallard and Gail Hale. Many, many thanks for your unwavering support of the archives and me. Your support and interest in the archives is one reason I love doing what I do.

George Hutchins, thank you for providing so much assistance in this process. And thank you for loaning me your collections of posters and clippings and time toward this project. This process would have been a lot more difficult without your help and support.

Helen Whittaker and the rest of the Kingsport Public Library and Archives staff, thank you all for your encouragement and support.

Candice Lawrence from The History Press, thank you for your guidance through this process.

Kari Roueche, thank you for being an award-winning volunteer, and thank you for everything. Words really cannot describe the amount of gratitude I have for you. Thank you for your friendship and encouragement.

Emma Lin, thank you for helping me with research and all the time you spent on the newspaper archive.

Jim Johnson, thank you for being an awesome dad. You have always been there for me with encouraging words and unconditional love. Without you I would not have had the support to become the person that I am today.

Teresa Johnson, my late mother, thank you for being my mother. I could not have asked for a better one. You will forever be my best friend. You are my strength. I miss you every day.

Mitch Wright, my husband and friend, thank you for your support through this process and through every aspect of this crazy, beautiful life we have chosen to share together. Thank you for saying "whatever you need" and actually meaning it. Without your support, I don't know where I would be. And thank you always for being such a fantastic dad to our Lily. I will be forever grateful to you for her.

And lastly, to Lily James Wright: You are my greatest gift. I thank my lucky stars for you every single day. You are my deepest motivation, and I love you.

INTRODUCTION

As the archivist for the City of Kingsport, I have been immersed in the history of this city for close to a decade now. From my first day on the job to now, the history of Kingsport has been fascinating to me. And luckily, I have access to that history right at my fingertips. The Archives of the City of Kingsport is full of documents, photographs and artifacts that demonstrate how Kingsport's history has been shaped. With the centennial approaching in 2017, it has become even more evident how important our community history is. It is time to celebrate all that came before for us and look forward to another one hundred successful and dynamic years. Kingsport's history as a privately financed and professionally planned town and just how all that came together is pretty incredible. The cooperation of industries and the spirits of the people who made this town are incredibly dynamic. *On This Day in Kingsport History* is my attempt to share part of Kingsport's dynamic history, within a day-by-day format. Through the 365 entries you will recognize some major events, well-known people and recognizable places. But I have also tried to present history that is forgotten, that isn't well known and may be even a little odd and unbelievable. All in all, the entries give a glimpse into a different side of Kingsport that I am excited to share. I hope you will enjoy reading this book as much as I enjoyed putting the stories together.

JANUARY

January 1, 1942

Day of Prayer

Many local merchants and businesses were closed today from 10:00 a.m. to 11:00 a.m. to recognize the proclamation made by President Franklin D. Roosevelt that this day be a day of prayer during which all American Citizens should pray for victory. According to his proclamation, "The year 1941 has brought upon our Nation a war of aggression by powers dominated by arrogant rulers whose selfish purpose is to destroy free institutions….Therefore, I…do hereby appoint the first day of the year 1942 as a Day of Prayer, of asking forgiveness for our shortcomings of the past, of consecration to the tasks of the present, of asking God's help in days to come." The request to honor the proclamation was made to the Kingsport Merchants Association by the Ministerial Association of Kingsport. The Broad Street Methodist Church held a union prayer service that members of any congregation could attend. The Maple Street Methodist Church also held a prayer service. Both churches remained open to the public all day.

January 2, 1943

First Traffic Death of the Year

Kingsport's first traffic death of 1943, and the first since July 1942, was recorded on this day. Around 5:00 p.m., James Howard Cleaton Jr., son of Mr. and Mrs. James Howard Cleaton Sr., was fatally injured when he was struck by a truck. Cleaton was crossing Market Street in the block around Wexler and Island Streets. According to the driver of the truck, Nathan Mullins, neither the speedometer nor the brakes were working. The vehicle was a dump truck being used on a local construction project. The Cleaton family had only resided in Kingsport for a few months.

January 3, 1985

The River Premieres in Kingsport

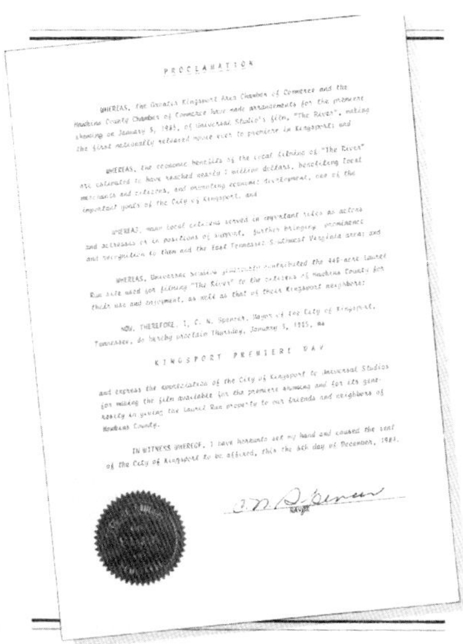

PROCLAMATION

WHEREAS, the Greater Kingsport Area Chamber of Commerce and the Hawkins County Chamber of Commerce have made arrangements for the premiere showing on January 3, 1985, of Universal Studio's film, "The River", making the first nationally released movie ever to premiere in Kingsport; and

WHEREAS, the economic benefits of the local filming of "The River" are estimated to have reached nearly [illegible] million dollars, benefiting local merchants and citizens, and promoting economic development, one of the important goals of the City of Kingsport, and

WHEREAS, many local citizens served in important roles as actors and actresses or in positions of support, further bringing prominence and recognition to them and the East Tennessee Southwest Virginia area; and

WHEREAS, Universal Studios graciously contributed the 440-acre Laurel Run site used for filming "The River" to the citizens of Hawkins County for their use and enjoyment, as well as that of their Kingsport neighbors;

NOW, THEREFORE, I, C. K. Spencer, Mayor of the City of Kingsport, Tennessee, do hereby proclaim Thursday, January 3, 1985, as

KINGSPORT PREMIERE DAY

and express the appreciation of the City of Kingsport to Universal Studios for making the film available for the premiere showing and for its generosity in giving the Laurel Run property to our friends and neighbors of Hawkins County.

IN WITNESS WHEREOF, I have hereunto set my hand and caused the seal of the City of Kingsport to be affixed, this the [illegible] day of December, 1984.

MAYOR

The River movie premiere proclamation. *Archives of the City of Kingsport.*

The River premiered on this day in Kingsport at the Eastman Employee Center. The movie, starring Sissy Spacek and Mel Gibson, tells the story of a struggling farm family in the Tennessee Valley trying to keep their farm from facing bank foreclosure, floods and other hard times. The movie was filmed in the Holston Valley area of Kingsport, Tennessee. The floods in the film were supplied by the Tennessee Valley Authority and the Army Corps of Engineers with water from the Fort Patrick Henry Dam. *The River* marked the first nationally released movie to premiere in Kingsport. The film was nominated for Best Actress in a Leading Role (Sissy Spacek), Best Cinematography, Best Music, Best Original Score and Best Sound.

January 4, 1950

Sprankle Gym Dedication

Nearly two thousand people gathered at Dobyns-Bennett High School for the dedication ceremony of the new gymnasium. The gym was named in honor of LeRoy Sprankle, former coach and athletic director of the school. Sprankle, considered the "Father of Kingsport Athletics," attended the dedication along with school and city officials and many former players. A plaque was placed at the gymnasium that reads "Sprankle Gymnasium, 1950, in honor of LeRoy Sprankle, who inspired our youth to better citizenship, athletic director, 1922–1943." A dedicatory basketball game was played between the Dobyns-Bennett High School Indians and the Science Hill Hilltoppers of Johnson City.

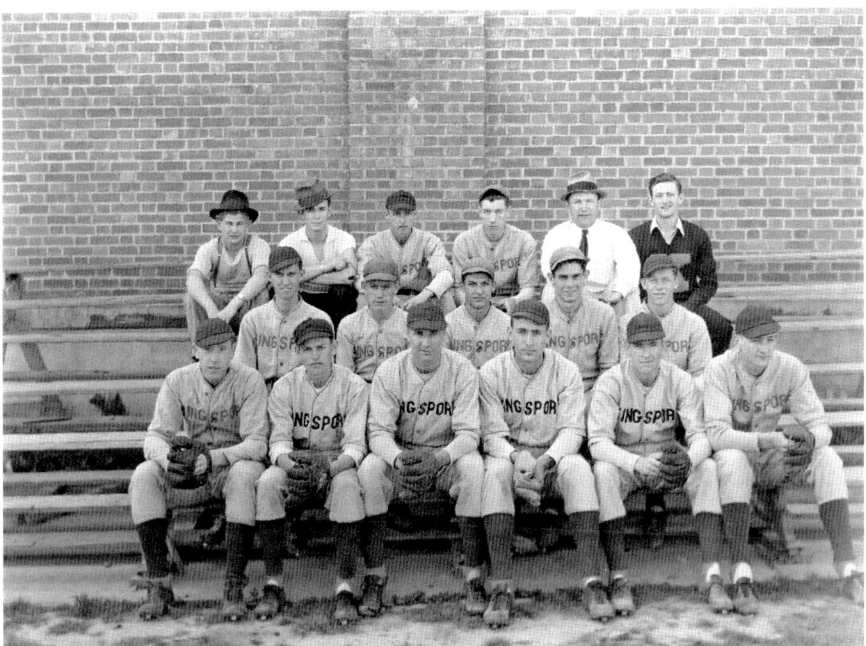

Kingsport baseball team with coach LeRoy Sprankle. *Archives of the City of Kingsport.*

JANUARY 5, 1956

No Union for Borden Mill

Employees of Borden Mill voted against union representation in an election supervised by the National Labor Relations Board. The final tally showed 444 voted against the United Textile Workers of America (AFL-CIO), and 337 voted for the union. Borden Mill was constructed in 1924 by the Borden family, founders of American Printing Company in Fall River, Massachusetts. The mill produced "gray," or unbleached, cotton cloth. Later in its history, a succession of owners operated the facility, including JP Stevens (JPS Textiles) and finally Chiquola Fabrics, which purchased the plant in 1999. The plant closed in 2003. Eastman Chemical Company bought the Borden Mill property in 2011, and the factory building was torn down in 2012.

JANUARY 6, 1963

Police Probe Mystery Death

Ernest Earl Adams of Dale Street was pronounced dead this morning upon his arrival to Holston Valley Community Hospital. George Stapleton, manager of a rooming house on Main Street, found his body around 5:00 a.m. Adams, an employee of McCrory's Department Store, was found at the bottom landing of a flight of stairs that lead to the second story of the rooming house. According to the initial coroner report, Adams suffered a head wound. Captain Broyles of the Kingsport Police Department reported that Adams was known to have been drinking upstairs in the rooming house and could have fallen down the stairway, but at the time of the initial report, it was impossible to say if Adams's death was a result of foul play or an accident. Adams, a World War II veteran, was survived by five brothers and five sisters. The funeral was conducted at Carter-Clamon Funeral Home by Reverend Ralph Cook, and the American Legion Hammond Post No. 3 was in charge of the graveside service conducted at Oak Hill.

January 7, 1946

Police Investigate Two Robberies

The *Kingsport Times* reported today that the Kingsport Police Department was investigating two robberies, one by pistol and the other by slugging. C.J. Ely, a local cab driver, reported he was held up at gunpoint by three people he had picked up in his cab. Ely was robbed of about thirty-eight dollars and tied to a tree, his mouth taped shut and his shoes taken. The three then fled in Ely's cab. The other robbery was reported by Paul Cloud. Cloud reported that two men knocked him in the head and took his wallet, which contained around eighty dollars. The robbery occurred in the parking lot behind Dobyns-Taylor Hardware Company.

January 8, 1972

Chief Warrick Dies

Tom C. Warrick, Kingsport's first fire chief, died on this day. His death was unexpected and occurred at Holston Valley Community Hospital, where he was undergoing treatment for a broken leg. Warrick came to Kingsport in October 1907 with George L. Carter to work as timekeeper for Kingsport Farms and in the general store at Rotherwood. Warrick was appointed to the first board of mayor and aldermen in 1917 by Governor Tom C. Rye. Warrick headed the first volunteer firefighting group when it was organized in 1916 and continued as fire chief for the city department from 1918 to 1935. In 1923, Warrick joined the First National Bank as an assistant cashier and trust officer. Warrick, a one-time deputy sheriff, also worked for Tennessee Eastman Company in the personnel department for twenty-two years. Warrick was a charter member of the Kingsport Kiwanis Club and the Kingsport Lodge No. 1385, Benevolent and Protective Order of Elks, of which he was elected the first grand exalted ruler of order.

January 9, 1947

Farewell Party

A semiformal farewell party was held in honor of Irene Crawford on this day at the Civic Auditorium. Irene Crawford was headed to New York to enter the Barbizon School of Modeling. The party, hosted by her mother, Mrs. Kate Crawford; Mrs. Raymond Cole; and Mrs. Lawrence Butler, featured a color scheme of green, yellow and white. Prior to the party a bon-voyage handkerchief shower was given. Crawford was gifted a "happy landings" handkerchief by Christine Larkins. The handkerchief was made from a piece of parachute that had saved the life of Larkins's uncle when he was shot down over Rheims, France. Miss Crawford, a graduate of Dobyns-Bennett High School, was selected by her classmates as the prettiest girl in the 1946 senior class. For a time, Crawford was signed with Hawk and Conn Modeling Agency in New York City.

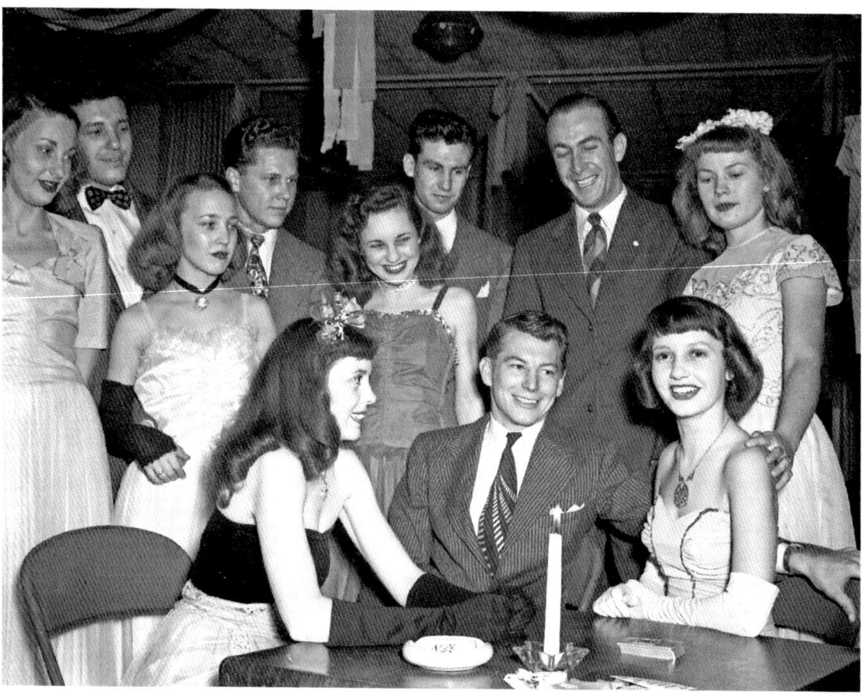

Irene Crawford's going away party. *Archives of the City of Kingsport.*

JANUARY 10, 1959

Book of Golden Deeds

Mrs. Ann Sindon, principal of Ross Camp Ground Elementary School and former woman constable in Hawkins County, attended a banquet in her honor hosted by the Exchange Club. At the banquet, held at Ridgefields Country Club, Mrs. Sindon received the Exchange Club's "Book of Golden Deeds" Award. The award recognizes dedicated volunteers who give endless hours of their time and talents toward making their communities better places to live. Sindon was also presented with an orchid, a trophy and a certificate. Her name is also inscribed permanently in the *Book of Golden Deeds*.

JANUARY 11, 1947

Swing and Sway with Sammy Kaye

Sammy Kaye and his orchestra provided the entertainment for the Civitan Club–sponsored dance at the Civic Auditorium on this day. Prior to the dance, Kaye and his orchestra played a special program from Munroe's Radio Shop. The program was broadcasted on WKPT, and afterward, Kaye met with fans and autographed records. Sammy Kaye was a leader of

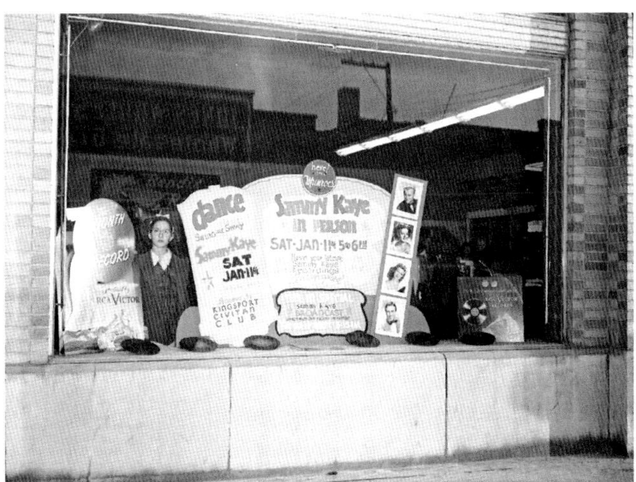

Sammy Kaye window display at Munroe's. *Archives of the City of Kingsport.*

one of the "sweet" bands of the big-band era. During his performances, he would often call audience members onto the stage to lead the orchestra. This gimmick became known as "So You Want to Lead a Band?"

January 12, 1941

Pioneer Resident Dies

Ben E. Dobyns, a well-known pioneer of Kingsport, died today around 5:00 a.m. at the Holston Valley Community Hospital. Educated at Milligan College and the University of Tennessee, Dobyns came to Kingsport with his parents, James W. Dobyns and Lula Lee Cooper Dobyns, in the early 1900s. James W. Dobyns served as the city's first mayor, and Mrs. Dobyns was affectionately known as "Mother Dobyns" around Kingsport. Ben Dobyns was a charter member of the Kingsport Kiwanis Club, a director of the First National Bank and vice-president of Dobyns-Taylor Hardware Company.

January 13, 1950

No Fear

Friday the Thirteenth? According to Mrs. Lucy McCorkle, so what? Mrs. McCorkle told the *Kingsport Times* that she had no fear of Friday the Thirteenth. To prove it, she brought her black cat, Mister, to work with her and stood underneath a ladder. An employee of the J. Fred Johnson and Company, McCorkle also wasn't afraid of the broken mirror lying near her desk. Mrs. McCorkle worked in the advertising department at J. Fred Johnson and Company, and she and her husband, Stewart, had one son, named Corky.

January 14, 1917

First Baptist Church Organizes

The first organizational meeting of the First Baptist Church of Kingsport was held on this day in a building at the corner of Main and Cherokee Streets. The present site of the First Baptist Church on Church Circle was a gift from the Kingsport Development Company, and the church's first building was built with funds provided by William Roller. As the congregation grew, so did the church building. In 1927, a new building was erected around the original structure, and throughout the years the church has continued to expand and add on to the structure.

January 15, 1923

The Kingsport Press

The Kingsport Press received its first production order today: 150,000 copies of the New Testament. The print job, placed by an East Coast firm, was officially designated as order number one. The Kingsport Press was under the supervision of L.M. Adams, president of the corporation; and Charles E. Mandelick, vice-president and general manager. The plant, then still in its infancy, was gearing up to be the largest book manufacturer in the country. The Kingsport Press also had plans to start printing a series of classic titles, such as *Treasure Island*, which would be sold at Woolworth's and available for ten cents.

January 16, 1956

Model City Motors Girls' Team

The Model City Motors girls' basketball team romped all over the Kingsport Press team, 51–14. Rosie Morris of the Model City Motors took scoring honors with 14 points. Maddux topped the honors for the Press team with 6. Both teams were part of Kingsport's recreation league. The Model City

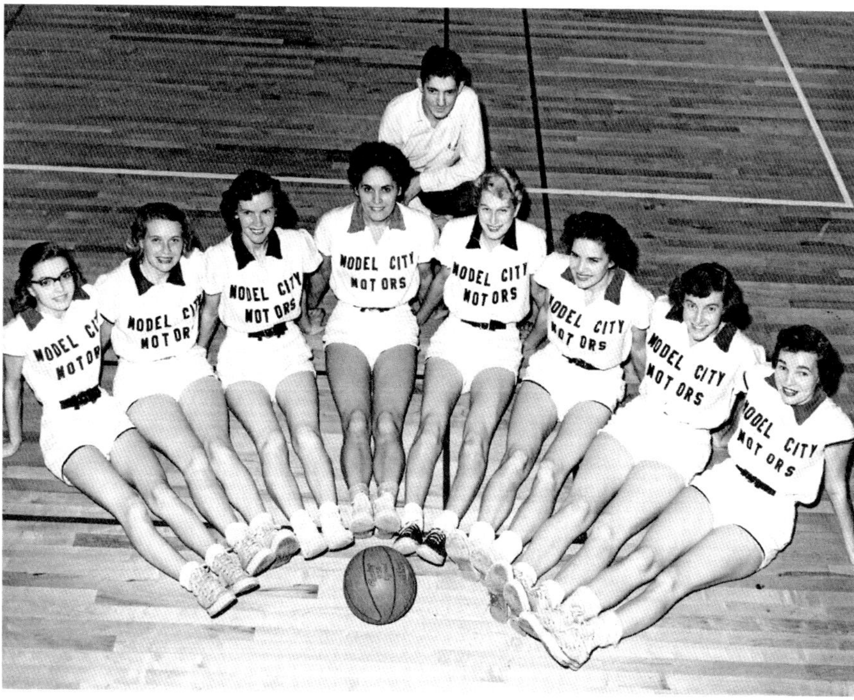

Motor City Motors girls' recreation league basketball team. *Archives of the City of Kingsport.*

Motors girls' basketball team joined the girls' city recreation team in 1953. At that time, they played against the Munal Clinic, Mead and Kingsport Press teams.

January 17, 1928

Joseph Herman Johnson on Trial

The trial of Joseph Herman Johnson, primitive Baptist minister, evangelist, rancher, piano tuner and confessed bigamist, began on this day. Johnson was on trial for the alleged abduction of Victoria Burger, a fourteen-year-old Kingsport girl. In August 1927, Burger disappeared from her home and turned up a nearly a month later in California. According to her, Johnson had come to her family's home and told her that he was an owner of a movie studio in Hollywood. The girl was convinced to leave Kingsport after

Johnson promised her a job in Hollywood. Johnson was tried on the sole charge of abduction, though he did admit in a preliminary hearing that he had been married five times without the formality of divorcing any of his wives. Johnson was sentenced to fifteen years in prison. Once the verdict was returned "guilty," Johnson remarked, "Damn, that's stiff."

January 18, 1949

Sunday Movies

Though the board of mayor and aldermen (BMA) approved an ordinance permitting Sunday movies, midnight movies would still not be allowed. The measure was first broached months earlier, when two different petitions were filed for the change. Kingsport joined other cities in northeastern Tennessee and southwestern Virginia, nearly all of which had Sunday shows. Sunday movies were to start fifteen days after the ordinance appeared in published form. The measure was endorsed by many civic clubs but opposed by the city's religious leaders. Reverend Edwin White, pastor of Old Kingsport Presbyterian Church, appeared before the BMA and called the proposed ordinance a threat to American principles of democracy. Reverend White said he was not opposed to people seeing good movies on weekdays, but he felt that the churches' wishes were being ignored by the board. He declared it more important for the churches to have influence in the life of the city.

January 19, 1972

Eastman Announces Expansion

Eastman Kodak Company announced today plans for an expansion involving capital expenditures totaling $316 million, including $73 million for Eastman Chemicals Division. Planned specifically for Kingsport were expansion of production capacity for textile dyes, a new plant for the production of specialty polyester polymers, additional steam- and power-generating facilities and the continuation of projects to improve the quality of air and water resources. The new plant building would enable the

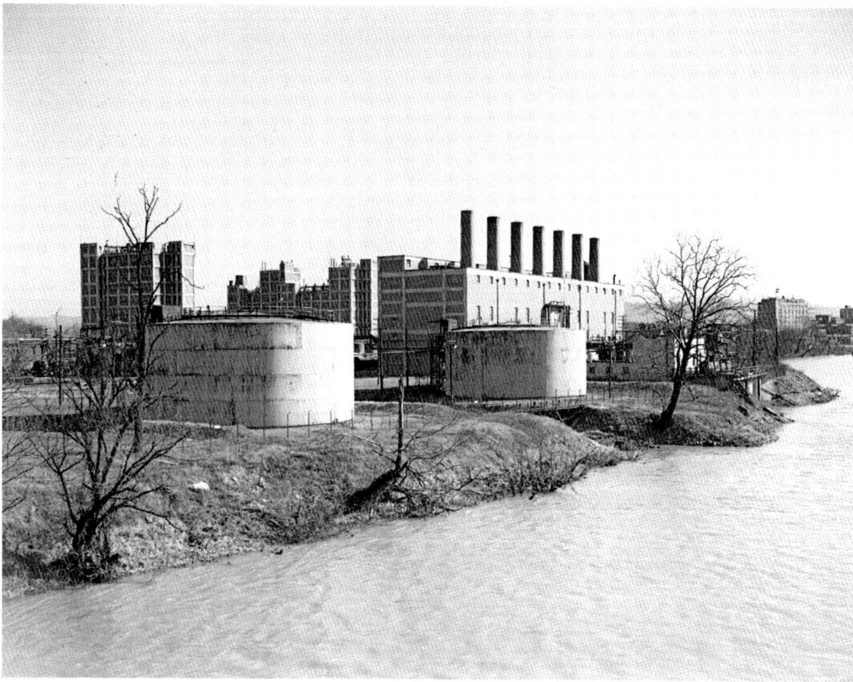

View of Eastman across the Holston River. *Archives of the City of Kingsport.*

company to make a wider range of products. In 1920, Kingsport was selected by George Eastman as the perfect plant site for Eastman Kodak. With its nearby forests and the Holston River, Kingsport was able to offset the shortage of raw materials available to Eastman caused by World War I.

January 20, 1950

Big Haul

Henry Dykes, proprietor of Dykes Store in Long Island, reported a break-in of his store. Dykes estimated the merchandise amounted to roughly $100. Listed as missing were thirty-three cartons of cigarettes, a case and a half of snuff, $14 in pennies (some in rolls with the store's name on them) and five or six dozen eggs. Dykes's business had been broken into before, about five years earlier. In that break-in, ten pounds of sugar, fifteen cartons of cigarettes and packages of soap were taken.

January 21, 2013

Presidential Inaugural Parade

The Dobyns-Bennett High School Band was chosen to march in the fifty-seventh presidential inaugural parade down Pennsylvania Avenue in Washington, D.C. The inauguration celebrated Barack Obama's second term as president. This marked the first time in the band's history that they marched for an inauguration. In 1926, Professor S.T. "Fess" Witt came to Kingsport from Norton, Virginia, to organize Dobyns-Bennett's first school band. The first band, composed of forty-five students, consisted of ten cornets, twelve clarinets, five trombones, two alto horns, six saxophones, three basses, two baritones, two drums, two fifes and one piccolo. Professor Witt served as director of the band until 1952. During his tenure at Dobyns-Bennett, Professor Witt laid the foundation for the excellence that the band program has since achieved. For many years, the students at Dobyns-Bennett High School honored Professor Witt with Fess Witt Day.

January 22, 1943

Gross Brothers

Roy Jevens, special agent in the technical laboratories of the Federal Bureau of Investigation in Washington, D.C., was to take the stand for the state during the murder case against Stanley Gross after the noon recess. The entire morning session was spent selecting the jury for the trial. Stanley Gross was accused of fatally injuring his brother, Lacy Gross, in a fight. The fight between the Gross brothers stemmed from a lawsuit brought to settle a fifteen-dollar debt for an automobile. Another brother, Andrew Gross, testified that he and Stanley were parties to the lawsuit, and after the magistrate's trial had been continued, Lacy and Stanley became involved in an argument, which led to Lacy's death. Lacy Gross suffered a wound to his temple and had minor lacerations on his hands and face. He was survived by his widow and two children.

JANUARY 23, 1941

HVCH Report

The board of directors of Holston Valley Community Hospital held their quarterly meeting at the hospital on this day. The board was informed of increases in hospital services during 1940, which had doubled and tripled the totals from 1936, the first full calendar year of operation. The greatest gain was a 218 percent increase in the number of babies born at the hospital. The board also discussed the temporary loss of three personnel due to military service. One was a laboratory supervisor, and the other two were resident physicians at the hospital. During the meeting, a resolution of sympathy was made to the bereaved family of the late Ben E. Dobyns, a longtime member of the board. Directors present were A.J. Agett, S.S. Benedict, Raymond Bennett, A.D. Brockman, W.T. Calhoun, Mrs. John B. Dennis, Mrs. George Earles, J. Fred Johnson, Mrs. Robert Meredith, A. Scott Noblin, E.W. Palmer, Max Y. Parker, Harry Sloan, Mrs. Walter Smith, W.J. Still and Mrs. H.G. Stone.

JANUARY 24, 1928

Dollar Day

Kingsport's Dollar Day, expected to eclipse all former Dollar Days in saving and sales, was virtually rained out. It was announced that many merchants, including Cates, Cincinnati Bargain Store, Freedman and Bornstein, Christopher's five- and ten-cent store, Arnott Furniture Company, S.L. Showkar Department Store, the Fashion Shop, Merry Garden, Dobyns-Taylor Hardware Company, the Miracle Store and United Sales and Salvage Store, would extend their Dollar Day sales for one more day. It is believed that hundreds of shoppers were rained out and did not get to take advantage of the special bargain offers. Kingsport merchants had been preparing for weeks to secure the best merchandise and goods for shoppers. It was decided to continue in order to give every person a fair opportunity to profit from the savings.

January 25, 1950

Modern Kingsport Settler Dead

The *Kingsport Times* announced the passing of W.E. "Uncle Billy" O'Brien, one of modern Kingsport's earliest settlers. Mr. O'Brien came to Kingsport in 1917 to work for the Kingsport Improvement Company. He was one of Kingsport's most active Masons, a deacon in the First Presbyterian Church and a member of the Rotary Club. He died at Holston Valley Community Hospital after suffering a heart attack at his home on East Wanola. He was survived by his widow, Mrs. Ruth Dobson O'Brien.

January 26, 1948

The Center Theatre Opens

The grand opening of the Center Theatre occurred on this day. The formal dedication was held at 9:00 p.m., with W.F. Winders as master of ceremonies. Prior to the dedication, the Dobyns-Bennett High School band marched through downtown, stopping in front of the theater for a concert. The theater was designed by architect Erle G. Stillwell and other members

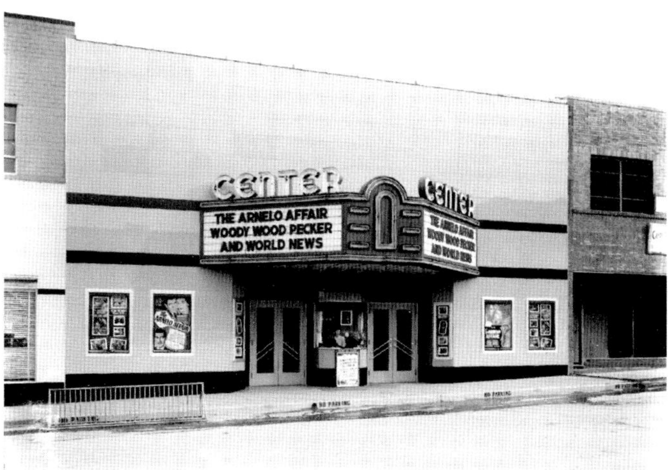

Center Theater on Commerce Street. *Archives of the City of Kingsport.*

of Six Associates Inc., an architectural firm from Asheville and Kingsport. The building, located at 119–21 Commerce Street, was constructed by W.R. Sproles. It opened with a showing of *Magic Town* starring James Stewart and Jane Wyman. The first person to purchase a ticket at the new theater was to a received a six-month pass. The theater was operated by Jimmy Pepper (president), Val Edwards (vice-president) and John Wimberley (secretary and treasurer) of the Tennessee Amusement Company. The Buddy Club at the Center Theatre was established a few months after the opening and provided entertainment for children.

January 27, 1920

Kingsport Music Club

A group of local musicians met at the home of Mrs. Joy Patton Thompson and formed what came to be known as the Kingsport Music Club. The object of the club was twofold: first, to advance the interest and promote the culture of musical art in Kingsport; second, to promote the mutual improvement of members. It was decided the club would hold bimonthly meetings and that programs would be held at each meeting. The charter members included Mrs. Hufford, Mrs. Geiger, Mrs. Whitcomb, Mrs. Thompson, Mr. Beatty, Mr. Davis and Mr. Dryden.

January 28, 1938

Palmer Appointed to Advisory Board

E.W. Palmer, president of the Kingsport Press, accepted today an appointment to serve as director on the advisory board of the Nashville branch of the Federal Reserve Bank in Atlanta. His term was to expire on December 31, 1940. In addition to being president of the Kingsport Press, Palmer was currently the vice-president and director of the First National Bank of Kingsport. Palmer served as president of the Kingsport Press from 1925 until his death in 1953. During his lifetime, Palmer was involved with over seventy civic and philanthropic organizations, and he served as deputy director of the War Production Board's printing and publishing division during World War II. In 1943, he received the rank of colonel for his work. Palmer was also awarded the Legion of Merit for his service to the United States during the war.

January 29, 1953

Nurses for March of Dimes

Starting on this day, Kingsport's active and retired nurses joined the March of Dimes to aid in the local polio fund drive. The nurses were stationed at the State Theater on Broad Street during the theater's run of *The Man Behind the Gun* and on hand to distribute envelopes in which a contribution to the March of Dimes could be placed. Joe Platt, March of Dimes chairman, announced that both active and retired nurses were recruited.

January 30, 1920

Indian Operetta

The Feast of the Red Corn, an Indian operetta in two acts by Paul Bliss, was presented in the auditorium of the Central High School at eight o'clock in the evening. The performance by the girls' Glee Club was conducted by Alice Feeney, school director of music. The chorus of singers and dancers comprised forty-nine girls and eight boys. Joyce Eckhart directed the choreography for the show, while Edythe Brownell was the pianist for the evening. Members of the main cast included Ruth Bennett, Hope Brown, Helen Black, Mildred Mahan, Opal Brandon, Margaret Kinzer and Woodrow Pickering.

January 31, 1924

Heavy Hitter

Former Kingsport baseball player A.L. Burton was acquitted of bigamy charges on this day. It was charged that he had a wife in another part of the country when he married a local woman. He was arrested in the fall and had been held in the county jail awaiting trial. He was immediately released following the not-guilty verdict. Burton, a catcher and outfielder, was among the heaviest hitters on the team. He played for the Kingsport Indians and the Johnson City Soldiers in the 1920s.

FEBRUARY

February 1, 1957

Youths Charged in Stabbing

Four Kingsport juveniles in the city jail today were charged with a felonious assault involving the stabbing of Hubert Lee Chapel Jr. of Hawkins County. One of the jailed youths admitted to the stabbing that occurred on January 27 in front of the Carter-Claymon Funeral Home. Chapel was taken to Holston Valley Community Hospital with a knife wound in his abdomen. He was listed in fair condition. City detective Jim Broyles and officer George Rogers arrested the youths involved at Ross N. Robinson Junior High and Sullivan High School. A trial date had not yet been set.

February 2, 1932

Deestrick Skule Up to Date

It was announced today that the cast of the *Deestrick Skule Up to Date* comedy had been decided and rehearsals begun. The play, directed by Miss Isabel Heuple, dramatic instructor at the Dobyns-Bennett High School, was presented by the PTA of Dobyns-Bennett High School on February 11.

The play was a humorous burlesque on the old-fashioned district school combined with the latest modern jokes and witty remarks. The plot centered on Professor John D. Rockefeller Dunsberry, principal of Coon Creek Hollow School, who runs the school in an old-fashioned manner. When the modern students arrive, they disrupt the school and anger Madame Okefonokee Shumanchink, the old-maid president of the board of trustees, who secretly expects to marry the professor.

February 3, 1960

Didn't Have Anything Else to Do

The *Kingsport News* reported on this day that juvenile court judge Roller sentenced two boys to indefinite periods in the state reform school for burglarizing the Sport Shop and breaking into at least fifteen parking meters. Don Castle, fourteen, and Danny Harrison, twelve, pleaded guilty to the charges. Both were under suspended sentences from reform school for larceny the previous October. The boys told Judge Roller that they stole two revolvers from the Sport Shop and had planned to rob a restaurant and then leave town. They changed their minds about the armed robbery because they "got scared." When Harrison was questioned by Judge Roller as to why he committed the burglaries, he replied, "I didn't have anything else to do."

February 4, 1957

Emergency Drive

S. Flem Dobyns, chairman of "Emergency for Neighbors," deemed the drive to aid flood victims in Virginia a success. The drive succeeded in breaking all records in the city's history. More than 300,000 pounds of clothing, food, bedding and furniture were collected. Thirteen truckloads had already been sent to southwestern Virginia. Three more truckloads were scheduled to be delivered by Mason-Dixon trucks. The drive had been halted for the time being, as the committee continued to organize donations and would assess further needs. The flood was considered one of the worst to ever hit the

Appalachian Mountains region. According to Virginia governor Thomas Stanley's telegram to President Eisenhower, "over two thousand persons were homeless…and many homes and business establishments were damaged by the floods." Southwestern Virginia was deemed an official disaster area.

February 5, 1924

BPOE Lodge

Kingsport Lodge No. 1385 of the Benevolent and Protective Order of Elks (BPOE) met in its new lodge in the Roller building on Broad Street. A number of candidates were to be initiated into the lodge at this meeting. Attendance at the meeting was expected to be near 100 percent, as members were pleased with their new home in the Roller building. The Elks planned to discuss a considerable amount of business pertaining to the club's activities in the coming months. The first meeting of the Kingsport Lodge No. 1385 was held in April 1920 with a charter roster of 33 Kingsport Elk members. The meeting was attended by 180 Elks from Kingsport, Bristol and Johnson City. The first officers chosen by the lodge were Tom Warrick, grand exalted ruler; Gary McChesney, esteemed leading knight; C.E. Brooks, esteemed lecturing knight; W.R. Burnett, secretary; W.R. Jennings, treasurer; and E.B. Wolfe, Dr. E.W. Tipton, W.M. Bachman and A.D. Brockman, trustees.

February 6, 1942

Harris Tuttle Presents Lecture on Color Photography

Photographers both amateur and professional joined the Tennessee Eastman Camera Club to hear a lecture in color photography at 8:00 p.m. in the employees' building at the Eastman Plant. The lecture was presented by Harris B. Tuttle of the Eastman Kodak Company in Rochester, New York. The lecture covered the Kodak minicolor process and the new Kodacolor process. Tuttle was an expert photographer, lecturer and author. Some of his published works include *Color Movies for the Beginner*, *History of Photography in Law Enforcement* and *Sunsets in Color*. The Tennessee Eastman Camera Club was formed to advance the interest in photography among the employees of Eastman. The camera club sponsored contests, hosted exhibitions and held lectures and workshops on various topics involving photography.

February 7, 1974

Eastman Promotion Given

Lynn H. Farmen was appointed the assistant director of marketing of the Distillation Products Industries division, Eastman Chemical Products Inc. In addition to his appointment, Farmen would continue as field marketing manager of Distillation Products Industries. A native of Rochester, New York, Farmen came to Kingsport with Eastman in 1972. Farmen graduated from the University of Rochester with a bachelor of arts degree in economics. The Farmens lived on Sheffield Street and had three sons, and the family attended the First Presbyterian Church. Farmen served on the board of directors of the Kingsport chapter of the American Red Cross. In December 1974, Farmen was again promoted, this time to director of marketing of the Distillation Products Industries division.

February 8, 1937

Youths Charged in Automobile Theft

Law enforcement officials in Sullivan County apprehended two suspects in an automobile theft case. The suspects, Ed Cunningham, twelve, and Willie Rhea Penley, ten, are believed to be the youngest arrested in this area for automobile theft. The boys were being held in Kingsport following their apprehension in Middlesboro, Kentucky, where they drove the vehicle. The car, which belonged to Carlie Strong, was parked in front of a local grocery store when it was stolen. The boys had to remove the cushion from the rumble seat and place it on the driver's side to be able to see to drive. According to Ed, when asked if he understood the seriousness of stealing the car, he replied, "We didn't steal the car, we just borrowed it to take a little trip. We didn't hurt the thing." Neither of the boys had any money, and they intended to drive until they ran out of gas.

February 9, 1954

Founders' Day

In observance of Founders' Day, the Washington-Lee Parent Teachers Association met at 2:00 p.m. in the Washington School Auditorium. The meeting was opened by Mrs. William E. Stone, president. In the president's message, Mrs. Stone called attention to a pictorial history of the PTA and biographical sketches of the founders, Mrs. Alice McClellan Birney and Mrs. Phoebe Apperson Hearst. Committee reports were given, and the meeting ended with a tea.

February 10, 1961

The Land of the Dragon

The Children's Theatre, produced by the Kingsport Theatre Guild and the Junior League of Kingsport, presented *The Land of the Dragon* by Madge Miller, directed by Mrs. Richard Clark, with Mrs. Homer Clevenger assisting. The production was held in the Dobyns-Bennett High School auditorium. *The Land of the Dragon* was presented with no scenery, only props placed on the stage by the property man, who was to be in full view of the audience. The narrative was outlined by the stage manager John Pauley, who stood just off stage. The costumes were said to be delightful, with a distinct Asian flare.

February 11, 1929

Hi-Y Club

Dobyns-Bennett High School added another school club to its roster on this day with the organization of the Hi-Y Club. The club, for boys, is for those interested in the moral, as well as the physical, side of life. The Hi-Y Club is affiliated with the YMCA, with schools around the nation having clubs. "Hi-Y" is short for high school YMCA. Eleven boys were selected for membership in the Dobyns-Bennett High School club. The members

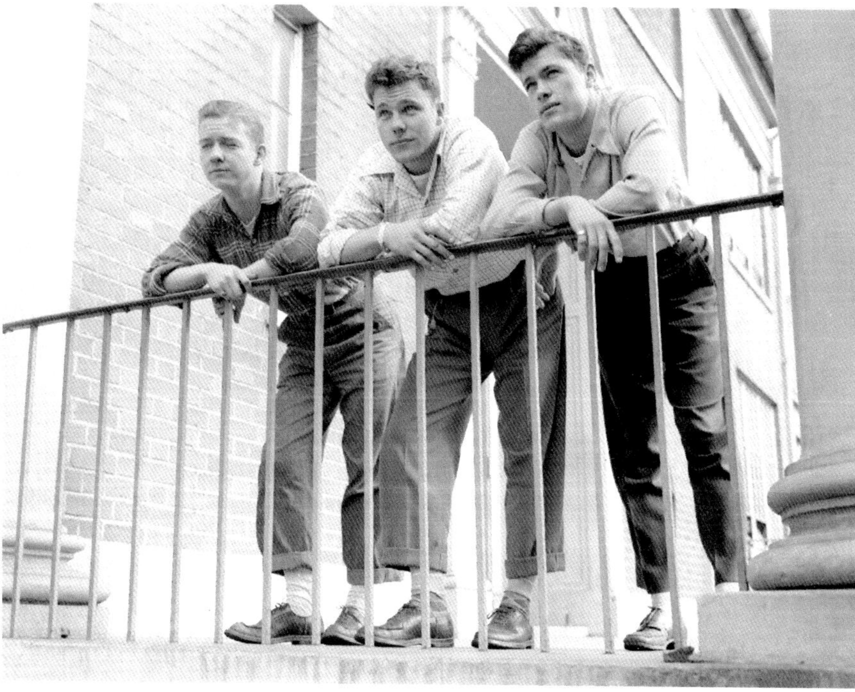

Members of the Hi-Y Club (*left to right*): Doe Hood (secretary), Kyle Shipley (president) and Bob Bingham (treasurer) 1946. *Archives of the City of Kingsport.*

were Arthur Agett (president), James Guenter (vice-president), Leland Smith (secretary), Ralph Morton, Holiday Smith, Wallace Hufford, Thomas Duncan, Erwin Ledbetter, Edgar Allen, Charles Keener and James Hamlett. Professor C.H. Nave, sponsor of the club, expressed the hope that interest in the club would grow and membership could be expanded within the year.

February 12, 1939

Rotherwood Dairy

For the second consecutive year, the Rotherwood Dairy herd qualified as a member in the Constructive Breeder's Registry. The notice was received by the American Jersey Cattle Club headquarters in New York City. The honor was highly regarded by dairy operators and only given to those herds operating on a so-called constructive basis. The basis called for continuous testing for the prevention of disease, official testing for milk and butterfat production and periodical classification for improved type. Two cows from the herd, Marionette and Gold Boutilliee, qualified for silver medals for having produced the required yield of butterfat. The Rotherwood Dairy started operation in 1927. The land, along with Rotherwood Mansion, was purchased by the U.S. Army in October 1942 during World War II for construction of the Holston Army Ammunition Plant.

February 13, 1947

John B. Dennis Dead

The *Kingsport News* reported today that John Bartlett Dennis, financier and creator of modern Kingsport, died at his home in Biltmore, North Carolina. Dennis, originally from Gardiner, Maine, was a Columbia-educated investment banker with Blair and Company of New York. It is through this company that Dennis provided financial backing for the establishment of Kingsport by directing the purchase and distribution of six thousand acres from the Carter Coal Company, which gave birth to the Kingsport Improvement Company. Dennis was survived by his wife, Lola Anderson, the first landscape architect of Kingsport and former manager of Kingsport Nurseries. The couple married in 1929. Lola Dennis died in 1969, and both are buried at Oak Hill Cemetery.

February 14, 1974

Vandalism Outbreak

An outbreak of vandalism involving a pellet gun started on this day and continued into the next day. When the spree was over, it amounted to around sixty-four cars damaged and window damage to at least seven business buildings around Kingsport. Two plate glass windows were broken out at Parkway Buick on Lynn Garden Drive. A window at the Tri-City Bank on New Street was shattered. The damage was especially bad on Tennessee

Street, where just about every car had been shot. Overall damage was totaled in excess of $3,000. Officers arrested two youths, sixteen and seventeen, on Saturday on charges of malicious mischief.

February 15, 1961

Holston River Survey

General Herbert S. Vogel, Tennessee Valley Authority board chairman, made a pledge on this day to conduct a new survey of the Holston River. The survey would look toward canalizing the river to provide transportation to the Kingsport area. The promise of the survey was made to a delegation representing the Holston Valley Improvement Association. It was advised that the delegation would be working toward Holston River Development through the Tennessee River Tributary Development branch of the Tennessee Valley Authority, which was headed by Richard Kilbourn. General Vogel emphasized that the date of the survey had yet to be determined and the actual work to make the river navigable was not on any current Tennessee Valley Authority timetable.

February 16, 1925

Conference Meeting

A conference meeting composed of the board of regents of the Riverview Hospital and Community Chest Committee was held at the YMCA building this evening. The meeting, called by Dr. O.S. Hauk, president of the Kingsport Men's Business Club, was to discuss the financial conditions of the Riverview Hospital and the Community Chest. A new committee was appointed to care for charity cases. Riverview Hospital was located on Netherland Inn Road. Years after the building stopped operating as a hospital, it was converted into the Boatyard Apartments.

February 17, 1974

No Satan at Central

Kenneth Goff, principal at Sullivan Central High School, put his foot firmly down on the notion of there being any kind of club at the school that studied Satanism. It had been reported that students at the school had organized a club called the "Satanic and Occult Symposium." The purpose of the club was to be strictly educational—to discuss, study and learn more about the subject. After receiving numerous complaints about "teaching devil worship" at the school, Goff wanted to make it clear that the idea of the club had been vetoed.

February 18, 1937

John Nolen Called by Death

Dr. John Nolen, internationally known landscape architect and pioneer in modern city planning, died on this day. Nolan graduated from the Harvard School of Landscape Architecture in 1905 and established an office in Cambridge, Massachusetts, where he and his associates branched out into city planning as well as landscape architecture. Nolan was the city planner who developed the plans in which the geography of Kingsport is rooted. Using previous designs and determining the needs of the city, Nolen created a city plan with areas specifically zoned for industrial, commercial, spiritual and residential growth and development. At one time, Nolen referred to Kingsport as his greatest accomplishment.

February 19, 1960

Kingsport Preaching Mission

The *Kingsport Times* reported that over five hundred people braved the weather to attend the Kingsport Preaching Mission event at the Civic Auditorium. The temperatures were frigid and heavy snow was expected, but this did not deter many from making their way to hear the Reverend Dr. Olin W. Hay of Louisville, Kentucky, and the Reverend Dr. C. Oscar Johnson from Berkley, California. The Kingsport Preaching Mission was part of the Appalachian Preaching Mission, a nondenominational entity that promoted unity among the various churches and provided an opportunity for the public to hear ministers from all over the country.

February 20, 1942

McAmis Home Fire

A fire today at the home of S.E. McAmis on Orchard Court caused an undetermined amount of damages, but luckily no one was injured. The McAmis family was on vacation in Florida when the fire occurred. According to fire chief Roy Pyle, the fire started in the garage and was caused by an electric motor that operated the garage door. The flames quickly spread to other parts of the house. The subfreezing temperatures made fighting the fire difficult, but firemen and neighbors are said to have saved a great deal of furniture and other items before the fire reached them.

February 21, 1951

Divorce Set Aside

Judge Webster of the domestic relations court set aside a divorce granted to a Kingsport resident based on grounds of perjury. The divorce was between William N. Mann and Bessie Jane Mann. In divorce court proceedings in November 1950, Mann alleged that he was a resident of Knox County and that his wife has deserted him two years before that. Judge Webster set aside the divorce after sustaining Mrs. Mann's petition that the allegations were false, on the grounds that both she and her husband had been residents of Kingsport for several years. The couple had been married for several decades and had five children.

February 22, 1935

Eastman Cagers to Play

The Tennessee Eastman boys' and girls' basketball teams would meet tough opposition this evening. The boys played the Fall Branch Independents, and the girls played the Elizabethton team. The lineup for the boys' team consisted of the following players: John and Arthur Brookhart, Bayard Williamson, Arthur Coffin and Fred Pollard. The girls' lineup featured Bernice Edwards, Wilma Conklin, Stella Baker, Luke Blankenbelcher and Margaret Walters. In 1941, the Eastman Cagers team consisting of Paul Schneider, Kenny Cantwell, Clyde Cooper, Kent Neufer and Claude Wright played an exposition game against the New York Celtics. The game, played at the Civic Auditorium, was sponsored by the Kingsport Civitan Club. The Celtics won 47–41.

February 23, 2012

Pal Barger Regional Center for Automotive Programs

A ribbon-cutting for the Pal Barger Regional Center for Automotive Programs (RCAP) was held on this day. The program, offered through Northeast State, was to provide an automotive educational opportunity for students. Barger, longtime businessman and owner of Pal's Sudden Service, donated $400,000 to the Northeast State Technical Community College Foundation to purchase the Free Service Tire and Auto Center in downtown Kingsport. The building was transformed into a facility to house the college's automotive services program. In addition to two classrooms and two offices, the center also contains fourteen workstations, four "virtual-paint" stations and a spacious shop area. Northeast State also received $25,000 worth of shop equipment from Dennis Powell, an automobile dealer and auto shop executive, for use in the Barger Center.

February 24, 1959

James C. White Honored

James C. White, president of Tennessee Eastman Chemical Company, was presented with the University of Tennessee's 1958 N.W. Dougherty Award at a banquet held at Ridgefields Country Club. The award is presented annually to an outstanding leader in the field of engineering. White, president of Eastman since 1945, was the second recipient of the award. The award honors Dean Emeritus Dougherty, who retired from his position as dean of the College of Engineering in 1950. White joined Tennessee Eastman in 1920 and in 1945, he received the Manhattan District special award for individual contributions to the Atomic Bomb Program. In addition to acting as head of Tennessee Eastman, he was also president of Texas Eastman Company in Longview, Texas. He was also chairman of the board and director of three Eastman Kodak subsidiaries: Eastman Chemical, Holston Defense Corporation and Holston Trading Corporation.

February 25, 1921

Everybody's Husband

The Kingsport Book Club put on a play titled *Everybody's Husband* that raised around $1,200 for the Kingsport Public Library. The play, held in the Central High School auditorium, was one of the first amateur productions to be produced in Kingsport. Many of the costumes were ordered from a theatrical house in Lexington, Kentucky, while some were made by the cast. Mrs. B.C. Sutton, a former New York actress, directed the play. Mr. Kingsport himself, J. Fred Johnson, was persuaded to be cast in the lead as the titular husband. Others in the cast included Mrs. Herbert Williamson, Mrs. W.R. Gilmer, Allen Dryden, Mrs. S.P. Platt, Mrs. H.J. Shivell, Mrs. R.Y. Grant, Mr. and Mrs. K.W. Koeniger, John Miller, Mrs. Henry C. Meeks, W.R. Gilmer and Mrs. F.M. Keller.

February 26, 1940

Gone With the Wind Premiere

The Upper East Tennessee premiere of *Gone with the Wind* was held at the State Theater on this day in 1940. Jimmy Pepper, manager of the theater, announced that the initial showing of the picture would begin at 7:45 p.m. During the remainder of the week, the film was to be shown twice daily, one a matinee showing and the other an evening showing. Reserved tickets were required and could be purchased at a special *Gone with the Wind* box office in J. Fred Johnson and Company. The film runs for three hours and forty minutes, not including the ten-minute intermission.

February 27, 1971

Rotary Club Suit Sale

This day marked the second day of the Kingsport Rotary Club's Suit Sale fundraiser held at Montgomery Ward on Commerce Street. The proceeds of the event went toward club activities that supported the Rotary Foundation, the Boy Scouts, expenses of the Rotary's district governor and the local Rotary Milk Fund. Rotarians were obligated to contribute two suits, clean, mended and with all buttons and zippers in working order, or they would be assessed an extra thirty dollars in dues. The sale boasted racks and racks of suits in all sizes, colors and patterns. All suits were on sale for fifteen dollars.

February 28, 1963

Fashion Show

Heart of Fashions was the theme of the second annual fun fashion show. The event, sponsored by the Appalachian Heart Association and cosponsored by Kingsport Alpha Nu chapter of Epsilon Sigma Alpha, was held on this day at the Civic Auditorium. Tickets for the 8:00 p.m. event cost one dollar, and all proceeds went to the heart fund of the Appalachian Heart Association. The fashion show featured free refreshments and door prizes, and the clothing was provided by W.B. Greene Company, Conley E. Morris, Jo-Ann, J. Fred Johnson and Company and Nettie Lee Shops, all of which specialized in women's fashion. The Kingsport Alpha Nu Chapter of Epsilon Sigma Alpha was organized in June 1950 with fourteen charter members. Miss Juanita Patrick was the first president of the Kingsport chapter.

MARCH

March 1, 1933

Douglass Tigers District Champs

The Douglass High School Tigers beat Langston High School of Johnson City to be declared the Ninth District basketball champions. The Tigers defeated Langston 23–21 in an overtime game. The score seesawed back and forth throughout the whole bout, leaving fans on the edge of their seats.

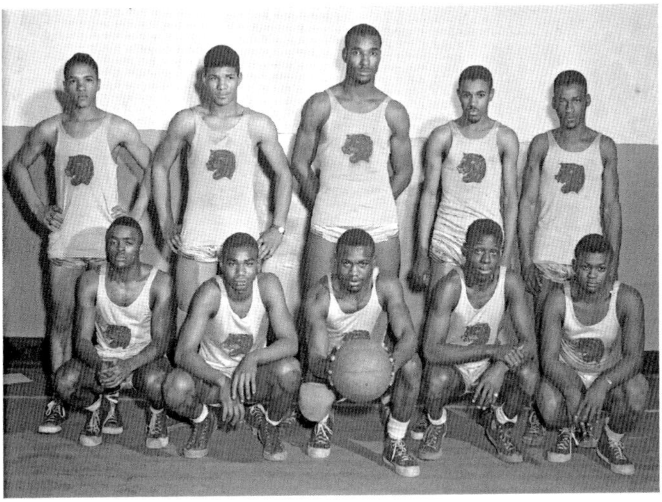

Douglass High School basketball team, 1949. *Archives of the City of Kingsport.*

At the end of second half, the score was tied 18–18, leading to the overtime round. Playing for the Douglass Tigers were Brown (4 points), Stafford (4 points), Lee (8 points), Horton (3 points) and Hawks (4 points). Members of the Langston team included Young (3 points), Cope (4 points), West (5 points), Leak (6 points) and Sherrol (3 points).

March 2, 1917

Kingsport's Charter

Officially chartered on this day in 1917, Kingsport became the first city in Tennessee to employ a council-manager form of government, with James W. Dobyns appointed first mayor. Kingsport experienced rapid growth in its first few years, and part of what made it successful was the planning of the city. Nicknamed the Model City, Kingsport is also one of the first planned cities in the United States. Kingsport's charter was drafted by Judge Hugh G. Morison of the firm Morison and Kelly, now Hunter Smith and Davis, LLP, in consultation with H. Ray Dennis of the Kingsport Securities Company. The draft was sent to the Bureau of Municipal Research in New York City, where Herbert Sands carefully critiqued the document. The charter, Tennessee Senate Bill No. 45, was sponsored by J. Parks Worley and introduced by Dr. O.S. Hauk. The charter was given final approval by Governor Tom C. Rye.

March 3, 1950

Fire at American Legion Home

This day's edition of the newspaper reported that fire swept through the home of the American Legion Hammond Post No. 3 on Pineola Street. The roof of the building was completely destroyed, as was a major portion of the building's superstructure. Mrs. Robby Reed, wife of the home's caretaker, was the first to notice the fire when she overheard a crackling noise that caught her attention. She was able to call for help from inside the house before safely escaping the home. The blaze appears to have been started in the attic of the house, previously occupied by the Kingsport Country Club. The American Legion bought the Kingsport Country Club Clubhouse and four acres surrounding the building from the Kingsport Improvement Company in 1943. The building was used by the Legion as a clubhouse and meeting place.

March 4, 1958

Mrs. Clifford Dead

Word was received in Kingsport that Mrs. John H. Clifford, widow of the late Dr. John H. Clifford, passed away at the Tusculum College Clinic, where she had been a patient for the last few months. Mrs. Clifford, the former Marian Janette Steele of Perth, Scotland, was a registered nurse who assisted her husband in medical missions for the Baptist Church. They traveled the world several times and served most of their time in the West Indies, Java and other islands of the Dutch East Indies. Dr. Clifford was chaplain emeritus of the U.S. Marines and the first secretary of the Kingsport YMCA. At the time, he was assisting Dr. T.B. Yancey in public health work in Kingsport. The Cliffords had two sons, Howard Edgar Price "H.E.P." Clifford and Gordon Clifford.

March 5, 1956

Downtown Fire

Fire damaged two downtown businesses, the Kingsport Office Supply and the Snack Shop. The building that housed the businesses was located on the corner of East Market and Commerce Streets. Both businesses were gutted by a fire that started around 7:00 p.m. in an alley trash box. Damages from the smoke, fire and water were estimated around $125,000 and $150,000. The adjoining building, Tranbarger Furniture Company, was damaged slightly by smoke. The Snack Shop was owned by George Karakas, and Kingsport Office Supply was owned by C.K. Koffman and S.E. McAmis. The fire took the Kingsport Fire Department over three hours to get under control with assistance by the Kingsport Lifesaving Crew. The building itself, owned by Mrs. George Buckles, suffered structural damage to the roof.

March 6, 1938

The First Lady

Mrs. Eleanor Roosevelt, wife of President Franklin D. Roosevelt, made a brief stop in the Tri-Cities. The American Airlines plane carrying the First Lady arrived at McKellar Field around 2:30 p.m. The flight, en route to Fort Worth, Texas, was scheduled to stop for roughly eight minutes to refuel. Accompanied by the Secret Service, Roosevelt was welcomed by a warm crowd of locals gathered at the airport.

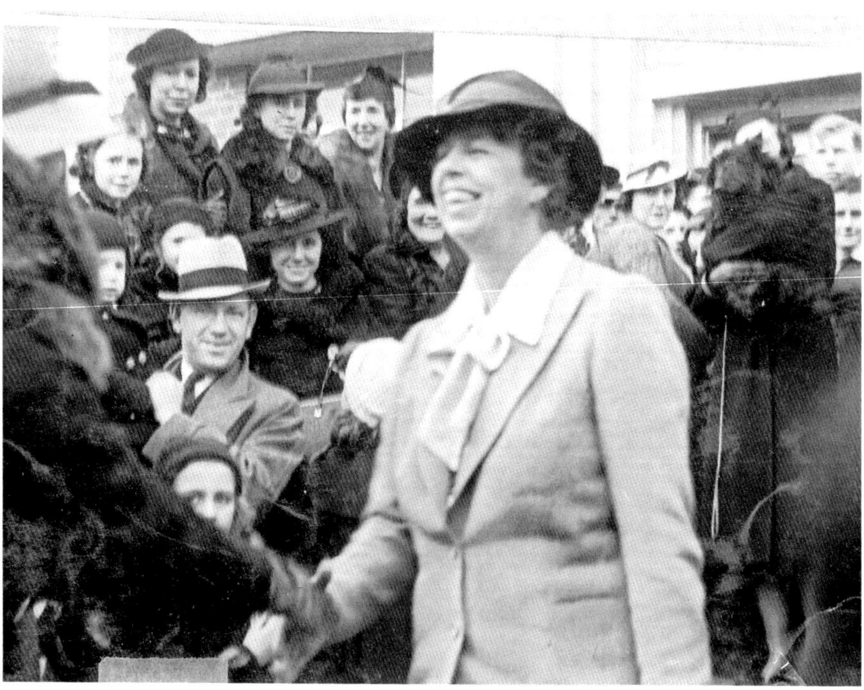

Eleanor Roosevelt at Tri-Cities Airport. *Archives of the City of Kingsport.*

March 7, 1942

City Mission Report

Thomas A. Williams, superintendent of the City Mission, gave an updated report concerning mission activities for January and February. According to Williams, the mission served 508 meals and assisted in the lodging of 283 people. Forty-nine confessions of faith had been made as well. He also reported that 12 unfortunate girls had been taken in, 2 babies were born at the mission and 4,760 attended services. The City Mission was located on East Sullivan Street.

March 8, 1943

Best Air Raid Control Center

Miss Nelle Major, field representative of the Tennessee civilian defense headquarters, was in Kingsport today to discuss with local officials coordinating state systems into a more compact and efficient service. While she was here, she inspected the Kingsport air raid control center. According to Miss Major, Kingsport had the best control center in the entire state of Tennessee.

March 9, 1958

Kinnie Wagner Dies of Heart Attack

Kinnie Wagner, legendary desperado, died of a heart attack while incarcerated in Parchman, Mississippi. The subject of the folk song "The Ballad of Wagner" was a legend of sorts around the South for his gunfights, prison escapes and the killing of at least five people. Wagner's killing began on Christmas Eve in 1924, when he shot Deputy Sheriff Murdock McIntosh to death in Greene County, Mississippi. Four months later, in Kingsport, he was involved in a gunfight with local officers. Kingsport policeman John Smith was killed. Wagner turned himself in the next day and was sentenced to the electric chair but granted an appeal. Wagner escaped and ran into trouble again in Arkansas, where he was charged with killing two brothers. He gave himself up to a female sheriff. He was returned to Mississippi, where he was sentenced to life in prison for the death of Deputy McIntosh. Wagner escaped three times, and during one of those escapes, he was on the lam for seven years. His body was returned to his native Scott County for burial.

March 10, 1976

Fort Henry Ribbon Cutting

Fort Henry Mall held its grand opening on this day. Local dignitaries and mall officials were on hand to cut the ribbon, and the Dobyns-Bennett High School band played for the crowd. The new mall, located on Fort Henry Drive, was 630,500 square feet, and an addition of 89,000 square feet had already been planned for next spring, when the JCPenny store would be built. Several thousand people attended the grand opening, but Charles Kinser had the honor of making the first purchase, at Parks-Belk, from manager Claude W. McInturff.

March 11, 1963

First Day of Press Strike

An estimated 1,600 employees of the Kingsport Press went on strike and set up picket lines before dawn today. Contract negotiations had been on hold since December 1962, and by March 1963 all negotiations had broken down. The main issues in the labor dispute were wage increases, vacation practices, reduction of the work week, seniority and manning of equipment. At noon today, W.F. Smith, chairman of the board of directors at the Kingsport Press, issued this statement: "A strike is in progress at the Kingsport Press Inc. After more than 100 collective bargaining meetings with the five bargaining units, the parties were not able to agree on some of the major economic matters. The plant is open for operations." The strike ended in April 1967, a little over four years later.

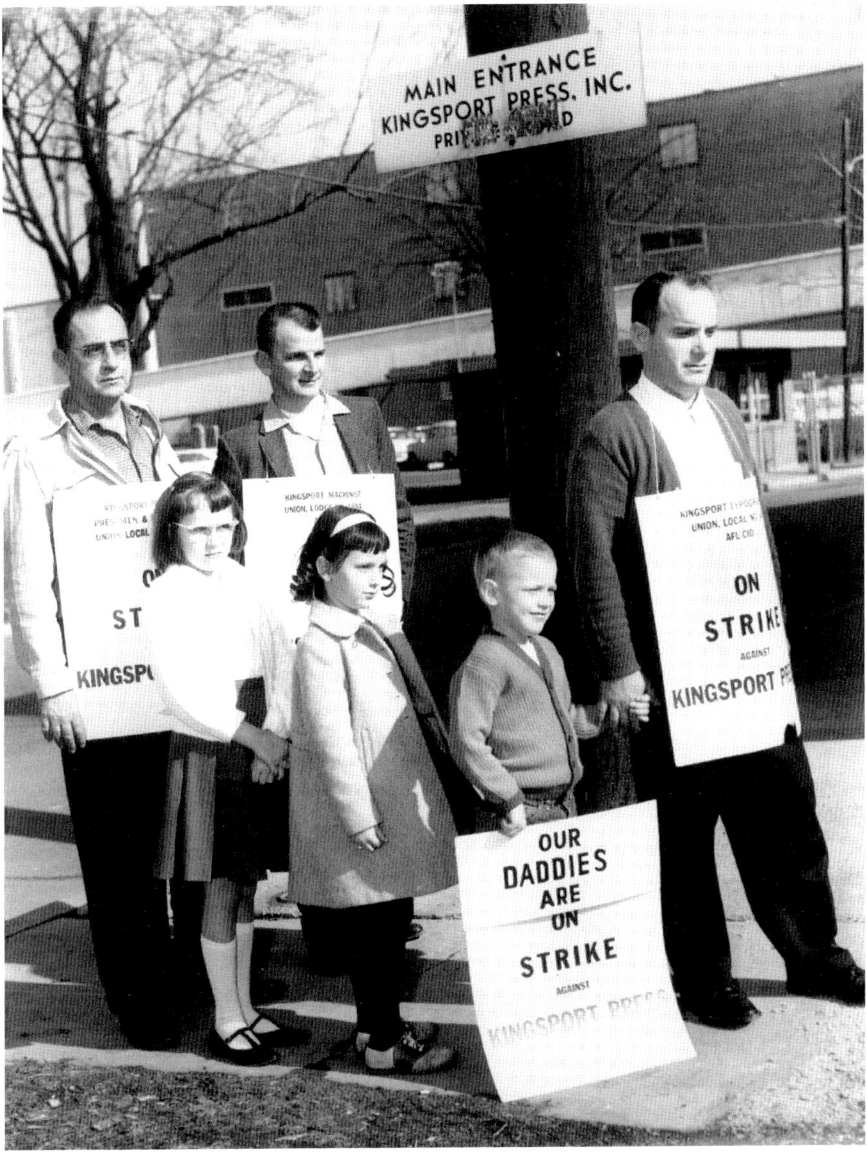

People holding picket signs, Kingsport Press Strike. *Archives of the City of Kingsport.*

MARCH 12, 1926

Old Kingsport Home Destroyed

The home of William Ramey in Old Kingsport was completely destroyed by fire between the hours of nine and ten this morning. All household furnishings, with the exception of a small bureau, were lost in the blaze. An employee of Mead Fibre Company, Mr. Ramey and his wife were not in the home at the time of the fire, but three of their children were. Luckily, observant laborers in the area noticed the flames and were able to get the children out of the home. It is thought that the family's cat was lost in the fire, as it was last seen scampering under the house before the structure collapsed. The origin of the fire is unknown and the approximate loss undetermined. The house was of wood-frame construction and quickly burned to the ground.

MARCH 13, 1927

Blue Ridge Glass

The *Kingsport Times* announced today that the Blue Ridge Glass Corporation had received its first big order. The local plant of the Blue Ridge Glass Corporation, which was gearing up to begin manufacturing glass on a large scale, received the order from another Kingsport industrial plant, the Kingsport Brick Corporation. The order was for several thousand square feet of ribbed glass to be used in the building of its new plant. The order also included all the window glass to be used in the entire plant, which would comprise three buildings. All of the materials used in the construction of the brick plant, with the exception of the steel, would be made in Kingsport. The brick used would be made by the plant itself, the cement used would be made by Pennsylvania–Dixie Cement Corporation and lumber and other building materials would also be produced locally.

March 14, 1933

Cherry Hill Tornado

A tornado swept through the Cherry Hill section of Kingsport around 8:30 p.m., leaving death and destruction in its wake. Both of Kingsport's hospitals, the Marsh Clinic and the Kingsport General Hospital, were at full capacity, and physicians and nurses worked through the night. The Red Cross and the Salvation Army established relief stations to handle the emergency. Some of the injured were treated at the Salvation Army, hotels and private homes. The tornado was said to have come out of nowhere, bringing with it hail larger than hen eggs that smashed windows and tore through the tops of houses and cars. Eight people were killed, and hundreds were injured. The Tennessee legislature provided $10,000 in aid to the victims.

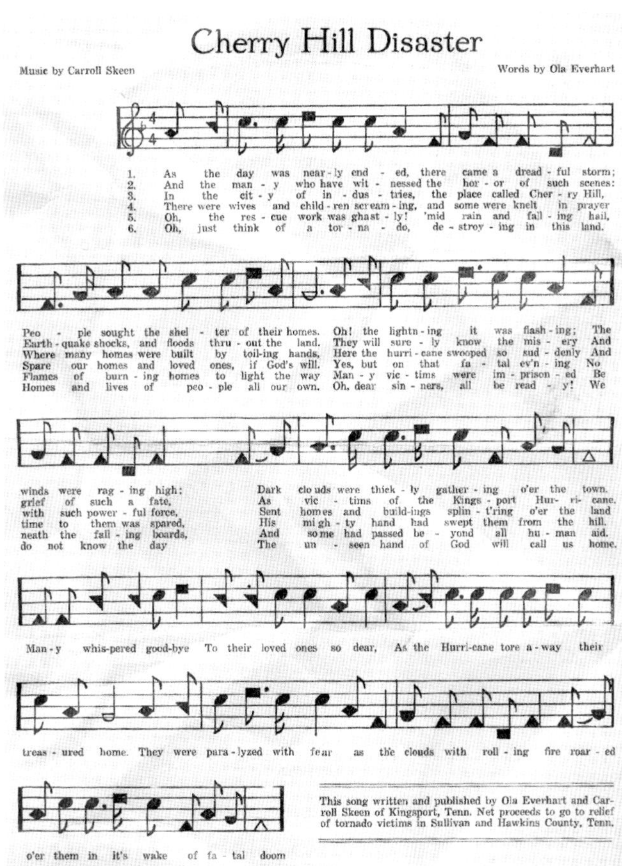

Cherry Hill Disaster sheet music. *Archives of the City of Kingsport.*

March 15, 1955

Horton Found Not Guilty

George Edward Horton, eighteen, of Long Island was found not guilty this afternoon in his retrial for the murder of Dewey Hobbs, twenty-seven. The first trial had been declared a mistrial when the jury was deadlocked after over seven hours of deliberation. Horton had testified that he shot Hobbs in a Long Island café after Hobbs accused him of breaking up his home and then started to beat him on the head saying, "Boy, why did you break up my home?" Hobbs's wife, Eula Mae, had received a divorce from the Chancery Court in Kingsport only a few hours earlier. Witnesses also testified that they saw Hobbs hit Horton and heard him threaten to "beat your brains out." Horton insisted that he shot Hobbs out of self-defense.

March 16, 1920

Cecil McCorkle Lives

The *Kingsport Times* reported today that Cecil McCorkle, twenty, lived. An employee at the Aniline Department at the Union Dye Corporation, McCorkle was believed to be dead, stricken by aniline poisoning. His grave had already been dug by the time he was revived. McCorkle was found unconscious in the boiler room of the plant; his father was contacted, and plans for the funeral were started right away. The grave had already been dug two feet down when word was received that McCorkle was not, in fact, dead. McCorkle had been affected by the poison as he was emptying an aniline tank. He was a new worker and had not taken the proper measures to guard against getting the aniline on his clothing. Dr. O.S. Hauk noted that McCorkle was rapidly improving.

March 17, 1955

Kiwanis Kapers Around the Town

The curtain went up at 8:00 p.m. on the 1955 edition of the Kiwanis Kapers at the Civic Auditorium. This year's show was a musical production titled *Around the Town*. The two-act production was performed under the direction of Larry Knowles. The first act included twelve skits, and the second act was devoted to *Minstrel via Mexico*. An addition to this year's Kapers show was the singing of "This Old House" by the Cavalier Quartet from Lynn View High School. The Kiwanis Kapers produced a community variety program for several decades in Kingsport as a fundraiser for the Kiwanis Club. The Kapers had a number of acts, from chorus lines to minstrel shows and a variety of various other skits.

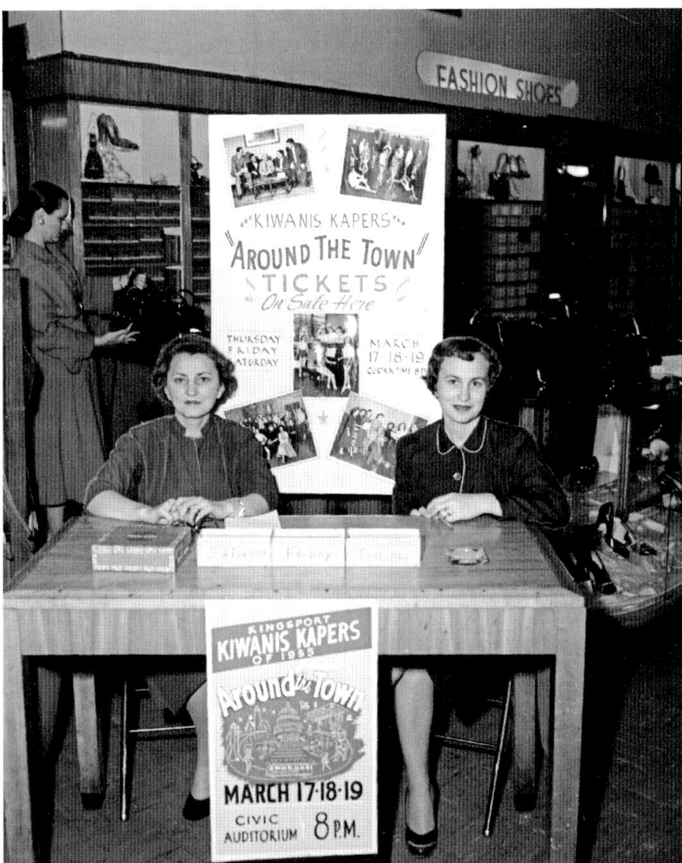

Kiwanis Kapers *Around the Town*, 1955. *Archives of the City of Kingsport.*

March 18, 1966

Damsel in Distress

According to the *Kingsport Times-News*, a damsel in distress was rescued by a knight in a shiny car after she became frightened by an apparent prowler. Brenda Rogers suffered deep gashes in her left hand from the sharp rain gutter along her roof. Rogers, who lived on West Park Drive, became frightened by an apparent prowler and leaped from her second-story window. She told police that she heard someone trying to get in the window and footsteps in the house. "Larry," a young man driving by, was able to catch Rogers as she jumped from the roof. Patrolman Billy Mitchell went through the house but found no signs of an intruder.

March 19, 1976

Spring Arts and Crafts Mart

The Spring Arts and Crafts Mart, sponsored by the Metropolitan Sertoma Club, got underway today at the Civic Auditorium. All proceeds were to go to the Speech and Hearing Clinic. The club also sponsors a Hearing Aid Bank that collects hearing aids not currently in use to test and repair and provide them on loan to those in need. The craft show featured pottery, wood products, paintings, candles, watercolors, metal sculptures, jewelry and leather goods. Participants included craftspeople from all over the country, as well as a few local and regionally known artists like Raymond Williams and P. Buckley Moss. Admission for adults was $1.50.

March 20, 1948

Buddy Club

The Buddy Club, sponsored by the Center Theater, held its first official meeting at 9:30 this morning. Jimmy Pepper, manager of the theater, had already registered 2,500 members for the new club. The Buddy Club was open to children up to sixteen years of age and designed to furnish wholesome entertainment, foster good citizenship and encourage clean living. Meetings would be held every Saturday at 9:30 a.m. with "Big Buddy" Pepper as master of ceremonies. All members would receive a lifetime membership card and a lapel button. The club's activities included birthday parties on the stage with cake, community singing and performances by talented children. In addition, there would be free balloons, candy and chocolate milk. The opening-day showing of the Buddy Club was the *The Thief of Bagdad*. A Hopalong Cassidy picture was scheduled for the next Saturday.

March 21, 1928

Law Court

Kingsport Law Court completed the hearing of the jury docket this morning and commenced the hearing of non-jury cases. Some of the cases completed were as follows: Ben King, caddy at the Kingsport Country Club, who lost the tip of his nose when it was struck by a golf ball driven by John Voller, was awarded $600 in damages by the jury. Dobyns-Taylor was awarded damages of $86 against C.H. Widener. A suit against Tom Foulk, involving damages from a car wreck, was dismissed. One divorce case was tried. Earnest Watson was awarded a divorce from Callie Watson on charges of desertion. The defendant failed to appear to answer to the allegations.

March 22, 1965

Yakely Bound to Grand Jury

John Yakely of River Street was bound over by general sessions court judge Walter Moody on charges of possessing over a quart of moonshine whiskey. A second charge brought against Yakely of disposing of evidence was dismissed. Deputies presented two and a half pints of what was believed to be pure moonshine as evidence. The moonshine had been confiscated from Yakely's home. Yakely testified he had less than a pint and argued that none of the deputies could be certain the whiskey presented hadn't been diluted;

he was released on a $500 bond. The whiskey was to be sent off for analysis to determine its exact content.

March 23, 1938

Heartbalm Suit

Mary Evelyn Lambe, jilted poetess and songwriter, was awarded $1,000 by a jury in Kingsport today as a result of a heartbalm suit. Lambe had sought judgment of $50,000 but was awarded the $1,000. Lambe filed the suit against R.N. Cregger, an eastern Tennessee Romeo, for breach of marriage contract. The case attracted a wide interest in and around Kingsport, with a capacity crowd appearing at the courtroom. Cregger had placed an ad in the *Kingsport Times* to help him find a mate and had been impressed with the letters from Lambe. Cregger proposed marriage, and they set a date. But Cregger ended up marrying someone else. Lambe claimed she was heartbroken and had loved him enough to marry him.

March 24, 1926

Attempted Suicide with Kerosene

It was reported in the *Kingsport Times* today that Mrs. Allie Miller was in critical condition in the Riverview Hospital as a result of burns she acquired when she attempted to end her life by setting fire to her kerosene-soaked clothing. The incident occurred at the home of John Hammond in the Lovedale section of town. Mrs. Miller had been a guest of the Hammonds for several weeks while her husband was in Florida. Prior to her husband leaving, he had asked Hammond if his wife could stay with him and his sister. He promised to send money for boarding his wife, but Hammond has not heard from him since. Mrs. Miller's two children had been staying with her mother. There was no known motive for her attempted suicide.

March 25, 1938

Kingsport Grocery Company Building Fire

The Kingsport Fire Department responded to a fire at the Kingsport Grocery Company on Main Street. The blaze was considered the city's worst in the past decade. Damages to the stock and the building were estimated at over $75,000. The fire was discovered in the rear of the third floor and spread rapidly to the second floor. It is believed that the fire started in the tobacco storage room. Although flames were confined to the third and second floors, the first floor suffered significant water and smoke damage. Hundreds gathered at the scene while the Kingsport Fire Department worked to contain the fire. Immediate restoration of the damaged stock and building were expected to begin as soon as possible.

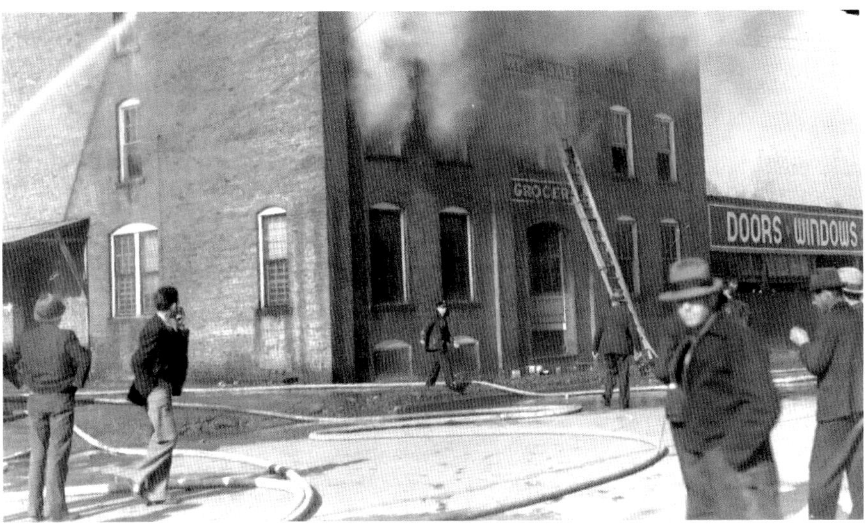

Kingsport Grocery Company fire, Kingsport Fire Department. *Archives of the City of Kingsport.*

March 26, 1978

State Theater Closes Doors

The State Theater on Broad Street in Downtown Kingsport officially closed its doors as a movie theater today. The theater opened in March 1936 with a showing of Bing Crosby's *Anything Goes*. The theater was designed by architect Erle G. Stilwell. The interior of the State Theater was designed by Italian artist Navino Nataloni, who was employed by the Wil-Kin Theatre Supply Corporation. After closing its doors, the theater was used as a dinner theater, a nightclub, a gymnasium and a cheerleading school. As of this writing, the State Theater has been undergoing a restoration for the past several years.

March 27, 1960

Last Sunday Meal Served at Kingsport Inn

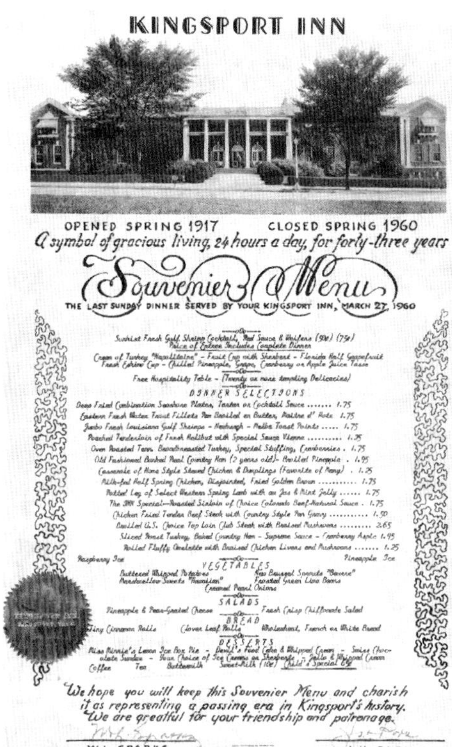
KINGSPORT INN

OPENED SPRING 1917 CLOSED SPRING 1960

A symbol of gracious living, 24 hours a day, for forty-three years

Souvenier Menu

THE LAST SUNDAY DINNER SERVED BY YOUR KINGSPORT INN, MARCH 27, 1960

Sunkist Fresh Gulf Shrimp Cocktail, Red Sauce & Wafers (90¢) (75¢)

Price of Entree Includes Complete Dinner

Cream of Turkey "Napolitaine" – Fruit Cup with Sherbert – Florida Half Grapefruit

Fresh Shrimp Cup – Chilled Pineapple, Grape, Cranberry or Apple Juice Tase

Free Hospitality Table – (Twenty or more tempting Delicacies)

DINNER SELECTIONS

Deep Fried Combination Seashore Plates, Tartar or Cocktail Sauce 1.75

Eastern Fresh Water Trout Fillets Pan Broiled in Butter, Maitre d' Hote 1.75

Jumbo Fresh Louisiana Gulf Shrimps – Newburgh – Melba Toast Points 1.75

Poached Tenderloin of Fresh Halibut with Special Sauce Vienna 1.75

Oven Roasted Tenn. Broadbreasted Turkey, Special Stuffing, Cranberries . 1.75

Old Fashioned Baked Real Country Ham (2 years old) – Broiled Pineapple . 1.95

Casserole of Home Style Stewed Chicken & Dumplings (Favorite of Many) . 1.25

Milk-fed Half Spring Chicken, Disjointed, Fried Golden Brown 1.75

Roasted Leg of Select Western Spring Lamb with au Jus & Mint Jelly 1.75

The INN Special—Roasted Sirloin of Choice Colorado Beef-Natural Sauce . 1.75

Chicken Fried Tender Beef Steak with Country Style Pan Gravy 1.50

Broiled U.S. Choice Top Loin Club Steak with Braised Mushrooms 2.65

Sliced Roast Turkey, Baked Country Ham – Supreme Sauce – Cranberry Apple 1.95

Rolled Fluffy Omelette with Braised Chicken Livers and Mushrooms 1.25

Raspberry Ice Pineapple Ice

VEGETABLES

Buttered Whipped Potatoes New Brussel Sprouts "Beurre"

Marshmallow Sweets "Hawaiian" Frosted Green Lima Beans

Creamed Pearl Onions

SALADS

Pineapple & Pear-Grated Cheese Fresh Crisp Chiffonade Salad

BREAD

Tiny Cinnamon Rolls Clover Leaf Rolls Wholewheat, French or White Bread

DESSERTS

Miss Minnie's Lemon Ice Box Pie – Devil's Food Cake & Whipped Cream – Swiss Chocolate Sundae – Your Choice of Ice Cream or Sherberts – Jello & Whipped Cream

Coffee Tea Buttermilk Sweet-Milk (10¢) Child's Special

We hope you will keep this Souvenier Menu and charish it as representing a passing era in Kingsport's history. We are greatful for your friendship and patronage.

Kingsport Inn souvenir menu, last Sunday dinner, 1960. *Archives of the City of Kingsport.*

The Kingsport Inn, designed by Clinton Mackenzie, opened in 1917 and became the social center of Kingsport for several decades. By 1960, the building was run down, and the hotel was closing. The last Sunday meal was served on this day in 1960. The last meal ever was served a few days later. Proprietors of the Kingsport Inn provided souvenir menus for the occasion so that people could "cherish it as representing a passing of Kingsport's history." The building was demolished shortly after.

March 28, 1924

Funeral of E.W. Dodd

The funeral of E.W. Dodd was held at the family home on Broad Street at three o'clock this afternoon. Dodd, a prominent citizen and businessman, died as the result of drinking bichloride of mercury. According to Dr. W.H. Reed, who was with Dodd when he died, said that all efforts to save Dodd from the violent poisoning death were to no avail. Dodd had apparently been in ill health and suffered from depression. Two weeks before his death, he had shot himself through the throat with a revolver and had fully recovered at the Riverview Hospital. He had been back home only a few days when he drank the poison that ended his life. Dodd was survived by his wife; a daughter, Ruth; and three sons, E.N. Dodd, John Dodd and Robert "Bobby" Dodd.

March 29, 1927

Floral Houses

It was announced on this day by the *Kingsport Times* that four greenhouses would soon be erected on the property of Dr. Will Hutchins in the Highland Section on the Bristol Highway. Orders for two of the floral houses had been placed, and work was to start immediately, while the other two would follow soon. The structures were to have dimensions of 150 by 30 feet and be made mostly of glass. Every modern and up-to-date detail would be considered in the construction. The organization of the company that would manage the greenhouse had not yet been decided at the time of the announcement. The greenhouses operated for several years until being closed down during World War II. New greenhouses for Hutch-Wallin Florists were constructed in the same location, just moved back from the highway, in 1946. Cecil Williams, owner and operator, handled wholesale and retail orders out of the greenhouses. The greenhouses were supervised by Ike O'Neal.

MARCH 30, 1963

Spring Dance

American-Saint Gobain hosted its Spring Dance at the Echo Valley Club. The featured entertainment of the evening was the Bill Salyer's Band, and the dance was held from 9:00 p.m. to 1:00 a.m. The price of admission was three dollars per couple and included a buffet during intermission. The Echo Valley Club was located in the Echo Valley area in Colonial Heights. The recreation club was a private club with a swimming pool, tennis and badminton courts and a clubhouse.

MARCH 31, 1948

Edgar Slemp Recovering

Every effort to save Edgar Slemp, fifteen, was being made at the Holston Valley Community Hospital, where he was being treated for a gunshot wound to the chest. The son of Mr. and Mrs. Ervin Slemp was found injured in a barn at his home in Surgoinsville. Edgar had used a .22-caliber rifle that he had taken from his home unnoticed, one that his father used for killing hogs. Edgar, one of thirteen children, was driven to the hospital in Kingsport by his father, who was an employee at Eastman. At the hospital, Edgar was given plasma and two blood transfusions. Some of the blood was provided by his father. A motive for the shooting had not been determined.

APRIL

April 1, 1921

Kingsport Country Club Organized

The Country Club of Kingsport was organized on this day with a charter membership of 125. The country club was located just south of the Bristol Highway on Pineola and just inside the corporate city limits. A member of the United States Golf Association and also the Green Section of that association, the club boasted many prominent members in Kingsport. There were also several women with memberships. The country club was controlled and operated by the Kingsport Improvement Company. Though golf and tennis were the principal features of the club, women often gathered on Saturday afternoons to play bridge or sew. The club also hosted various other social functions in the clubhouse.

April 2, 1954

Bogus War Hero Attempts Suicide

Thomas Owens, exposed as a fake Korean War hero, attempted to end his life on this day in the Kingsport City Jail. Owens swallowed the contents of a two-and-a-half-ounce bottle of disinfectant. His would-be suicide note read, "I, Thomas Tim Taylor, am writing this so you will know that I kill myself for I don't want to go on living anymore. Please send body to Kings Mountain, North Carolina. Signed Tim Taylor…Earl Owens." The plan didn't work, since what he drank was a new formula of the disinfectant that was nonpoisonous. He was rushed to the Holston Valley Community Hospital, where doctors said he would be sick but fine. Owens claimed he was a repatriated Korean War prisoner and had been awarded the Congressional Medal of Honor by President Eisenhower. It was discovered that this was not true and ended in Owens being arrested.

April 3, 1964

Model City Coin Club of Kingsport

The Model City Coin Club of Kingsport held its first coin show today at the Civic Auditorium, from 9:00 a.m. to 10:00 p.m. The show featured rare coins and paper money and included a rare coin auction open to coin collectors and any interested persons. Admission to the coin show was free, and door prizes were given away. In conjunction with the Model City Coin Club coin show, the First National Bank had an exhibit on counterfeit money, old coins and real currency. The exhibit, held in the bank's lobby, encouraged visitors to try to determine which money was fake and which was real.

April 4, 1960

Masked Intruder

The *Kingsport Times* relayed an interesting story this morning on a masked intruder in Mayor L.P. Gregory's home. According to the report, Mrs. Gregory was awakened by the sound of footsteps. She immediately woke up her husband and stated, "I think there is someone in this room." Mayor Gregory switched on a light, and there stood a man with a handkerchief over his face. Mayor Gregory leaped out of bed in pursuit, but the intruder was able to escape. Police arrived at the scene in minutes, but the masked man eluded them. L.P. Gregory served on the Kingsport Board of Mayor and Aldermen for seven years, including a term as vice-mayor (1957–59) and a term as mayor (1959–61). Gregory, a native of Jonesville, North Carolina, came to Kingsport in 1935. He owned and operated Gregory's Appliance until the mid-1960s. He was also president of Community Chest and chairman of the Kingsport Housing Authority for a number of years. Gregory was an active member of First Baptist Church for seventy-five years, and he died on January 13, 2008.

April 5, 1922

Newsboy Dies at Home

Little Eugene "Elmo" Nowfell died around 12:30 p.m. following an illness of three weeks. He was ten years and seven months old. The son of John and Gamala Nowfell, Elmo was a popular newsboy for the *Kingsport Times*. He was known to have a loveable disposition and unfailing cheerfulness. The funeral service was conducted by the First Baptist Church. Elmo was survived by his parents and a six-year-old sister. Elmo's body was removed from the Kingsport City Cemetery about nine months later and reinterred at a cemetery in Charlotte, North Carolina, by S.O. Haney, a former business associate of Mr. Nowfell's. His remains were placed with those of two of the Nowfells' other children.

April 6, 1936

City Mission

The City Mission, organized by the Reverend Thomas A. Williams and his wife, Clara, opened its doors on this day in 1936. Known for its location on East Sullivan Street, the mission originally opened in a building on Dale and Center Streets. The mission provided meals, lodging and assistance to anyone who needed it, from homeless families to wayward girls. The mission also held a church service every day of the week and often featured visiting pastors from area churches. Mr. Williams came to Kingsport in

1917 and started working as a barber in Woody's Barber Shop in Five Points. Mrs. Williams joined him shortly after from their native home of Butler, Tennessee. They met when he worked as a barber in her father's barbershop. The two opened the Magic City Barber Shop and the Clara Beauty Shop but closed them to start the City Mission. The mission served Kingsport for several decades.

April 7, 1922

Clean Teeth for All

Dr. T.B. Yancey, through the City Health Department, announced that Dr. Will Hutchins, a local dentist, had volunteered to clean the teeth of every child in the Kingsport city schools and in the public schools in the neighborhood surrounding Kingsport absolutely free of charge. Dr. Hutchins would be giving lectures in all of the schools and handing out cards to each child; presentation of this card at his office would get their teeth cleaned and examined. In addition to his duties as a local dentist, Dr. Hutchins was active in many civic and business affairs around Kingsport.

April 8, 1929

City Baseball League

The organization of the City Baseball League would be complete by the end of the day. Representatives from five teams and the officers of the league were expected to attend a meeting at the municipal building to discuss the league. President Harry L. Garrett and secretary Stoney Smallwood were working on a schedule, and when complete, it would be turned over for review and adoption. The five teams that had already signed up were King Motor Company, the Kingsport City Team, Kingsport Press, Holliston Mills and Borden Mill. The games would be played at the old city baseball field, Borden Mill and the high school, if possible. The time for starting the games had not yet been decided.

April 9, 1950

Ole Diz

"Never been in Kingsport before, folks, but I've sure heard a lot about all this fine country." Those are the words expressed by Jerome Herman Dean, or Dizzy Dean as he was more commonly known. Dean, an American professional baseball player, was in Kingsport to air his "Game of the Day" program. Over one hundred fans were on hand for pictures and autographs when Dean landed the night before at the Tri-Cities Airport. His "Game of the Day" program would air a big-league exhibition game between the Cleveland Indians and the New York Giants. The Giants beat the Indians 7–6 before the biggest ball crowd in Kingsport's history.

April 10, 1920

Billy Sunday

Evangelist Bill Sunday appeared before an over-capacity crowd at the Central High School Auditorium. Dr. J.H. Clifford briefly introduced Sunday, who spoke on Psalm 23. Clifford declared that Sunday "had come on a righteous journey over Sullivan County's unrighteous roads." Sunday's appearance in Kingsport was attributed to J. Fred Johnson, who attended a sermon of Sunday's in Bristol earlier in the week and convinced Sunday to come preach in Kingsport. Bob Matthews, Sunday's piano player, stated, "I don't know what came over him when Mr. Johnson spoke to him last Tuesday night at the tabernacle. It must have been that persuasive way Mr. Johnson had about him." Sunday, a former atheist and professional baseball player, converted to Christianity during the 1880s. Sunday was one of the most celebrated and influential American evangelists during the first two decades of the twentieth century.

April 11, 1968

Glen Bruce Park Dedicated

The Glen Bruce Park was dedicated on this day, a project for Kingsport's fiftieth anniversary. Glen Bruce, for whom the park is named, was one of Kingsport's pioneer settlers. A native of Wise County, Bruce came to Kingsport in 1915. He began working for the Kingsport Brick Company, and it was not long before he became one of its executives. Years later, he became the president of General Shale. Bruce served on the BMA as both an alderman and mayor. The park was built with local funds and contributions, a beautification grant and a grant from the U.S. Department of Housing and Urban Development. The dedication of the park was presented by Joe Worley with acceptance for the city by T.M. Divine, vice-mayor. Mrs. John B. Dennis activated the founder's fountain, completed at the same time as the park.

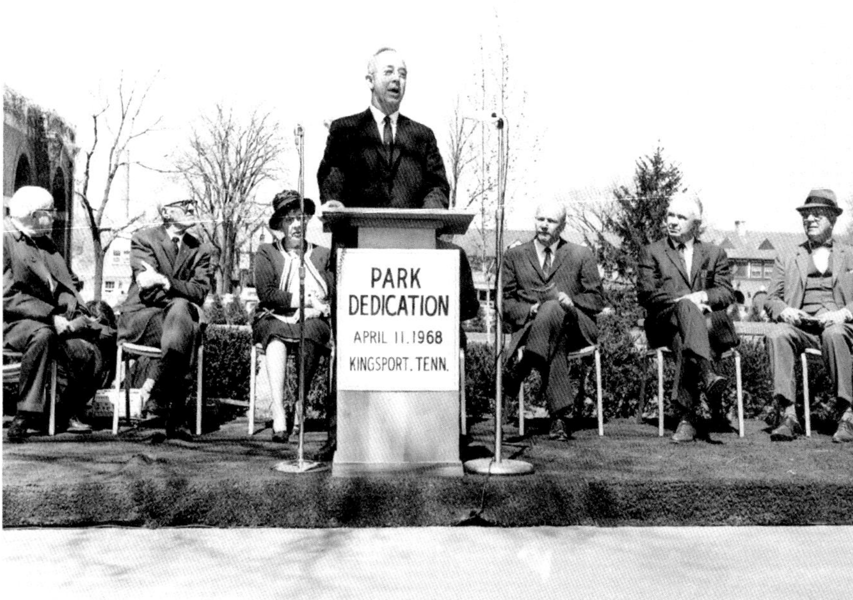

Glen Bruce Park dedication. *Archives of the City of Kingsport.*

April 12, 1948

General Shale Corporation Accident

Calvin C. Crumley of Reedy Creek Road was fatally injured in a dirt slide at the General Shale Corporation plant. Another man, Crumley's assistant, narrowly escaped the same fate. He had just stepped outside the pit to get a drink of water when the slide occurred. Crumley, an employee of General Shale for three years, was working alone in the bottom of a sloping excavation that the firm used to obtain materials for bricks. The earth caved in around him, burying him beneath dirt and shale. It took several minutes to unearth him before he could be rushed to Holston Valley Community Hospital. Rescue efforts were unable to save Crumley, and he died of suffocation after arriving at the hospital.

April 13, 1925

Officers Killed

Deputy Sheriff Hubert Webb and policeman John Smith were shot to death and policeman George Frazier wounded after a gunfight with fugitive Kinnie Wagner. Wagner, wanted for crimes in Mississippi, was engaged in a gun battle on the banks of the Holston River just below the Old Kingsport underpass. After the shooting, Wagner stole a horse from Dewey Nelson at gunpoint and was seen headed toward the Cherry Hill section of Kingsport. Wagner surrendered shortly afterward. Following a trial in Sullivan County that ended in a death sentence, Wagner staged a successful escape from state prison. He fled to Mexico but returned to the United States. He killed two men in Arkansas and turned himself in to Sheriff Lily Barber, widow of a slain sheriff. It was rumored that she refused to try him because she fell in love with him. Wagner was sent back to Mississippi.

April 14, 1950

State Department Movie

The *Kingsport Times* provided an update today on the State Department's motion picture of Kingsport made about a year earlier. The film, made by Knickerbocker Productions Inc. of New York City, would be finished "in the near future." The filming began in May 1949 and was scheduled to be approximately twenty-five minutes long. Intended for overseas distribution as part of the State Department's "Voice of America" Program, the film depicts day-to-day life in Kingsport as representative of a typical American community. In 2005, the Friends of the Archives of the City of Kingsport sponsored the conversion of an old 16-millimeter film reel of the movie to VHS and DVD and sold the copies as a fundraiser for the group.

April 15, 1946

Air Mail Service

Howard Long, Kingsport postmaster, announced today that there would be an opening of an additional daily air mail flight from the Tri-Cities Airport. The new flight, inaugurated by Pennsylvania Central Airlines, would originate in New York, stop in the Tri-Cities and then complete the route to Birmingham, Alabama. American Airlines would continue to operate its daily air mail service. With the new schedule, the Kingsport post office would be adding another messenger trip to carry the mail to and from the airport. Mail picked up by the evening planes would be distributed the next morning. Howard Long served as Kingsport's postmaster for twenty-one years. Long also worked as the vice-president and editor of the *Kingsport Times* for many years. In 1928, Long authored the book *Kingsport—A Romance of Industry*, published by the Sevier Press and printed by the Kingsport Press using paper made by the Meade Fibre Company.

April 16, 1920

War on Rats

It was announced today in the *Kingsport Times* that Kingsport would wage war on rats starting the following week. City health officer Dr. T.B. Yancey would be leading a "poison campaign" against the rats, as the city was in the midst of a cleanup campaign. Boy Scouts distributed literature on the correct ways to administer barium carbonate, available at any drugstore, to properly exterminate the rats. The cleanup campaign had been ongoing, and on this morning, the city hauled off four wagons and motor trucks of rubbish from the general residential area of Kingsport. Following the cleanup campaign, Dr. Yancey initiated a rat tail contest in which prizes were awarded for the most rat tails brought in to his office. The contest was part of the plan to rid Kingsport of its rodent problem. Ten dollars in gold was offered to the girl bringing in the greatest number of tails, while the boy bringing in the greatest number would be awarded a Winchester rifle.

April 17, 1959

Mock Nuclear Attack

Kingsport, as part of a nationwide civil defense exercise, was the object of a mock nuclear aerial attack at 1:00 p.m. today. The warning for the attack was received at 11:30 a.m. by civil defense director Jim Welch. Welch and other civil defense officers immediately sprang into action. Stations had been set up to broadcast, in code, messages of importance. Kingsport's code designation was Cherokee. The airwaves broadcast warnings that the attack was not real—it was only a drill—but the goal was to act as if the city really were under attack. Schools were evacuated, and volunteer families reported to the Civic Auditorium. There were mock attacks of varying sizes all over Tennessee today.

April 18, 1925

Cartwright Acquitted

B.C. Cartwright was acquitted of murder charges against him stemming from the shooting of a man named Neely inside the Strand Theatre. Cartwright and Neely had an altercation over the collection of tickets. Cartwright was a ticket collector in the balcony at the Strand and worked during the day as a mail guard for postmaster J.L. Shoun. Cartwright was carrying a pistol that he and his defense contended fell out of its holster, causing it to discharge and shoot Neely. Neely was first taken to the offices of Drs. Reed and Tipton and then later taken to the hospital where an operation was performed by Dr. Tipton, Dr. Reed and Dr. Keener. No measures could save Neely. The defense introduced witnesses that claimed to have seen the spark of the gun from the floor. This, and the fact that witnesses heard Neely say that Cartwright had not shot him intentionally, led to the acquittal.

April 19, 1954

Dr. G.W. Earles Dead

Dr. G.W. Earles Sr., one of Kingsport's earliest druggists, died at Holston Valley Community Hospital. Dr. Earles was survived by his widow, Jane "Janie" Pendleton Earles; and sons, Dr. George W. Earles Jr. and Dr. Howard P. Earles. Earles was a registered pharmacist in Tennessee and Virginia. He attended the Medical College of Virginia School of Pharmacy and came to Kingsport in 1920 to manage the Kingsport Drug Store on Main Street. He later became affiliated with the Holston Drug Store and, in 1941, opened Earles Drug Store on Center Street between Broad and Commerce Streets. After Earles's death, Janie Earles, along with George and Howard, continued to run the business. In 1960, Earles Drug moved to the corner of Center and Shelby Streets and featured Kingsport's first prescription drive-in window. Janie Earles was active in politics and organized the first Republican women's group in Sullivan County. In 1963, she was listed in *Who's Who Among American Women*.

April 20, 1939

Frank Wright Dies

Frank Wright, a pioneer citizen of Kingsport, died on this day. Wright was born in Montreal, Canada, to Captain and Mrs. James Wright. He came to Kingsport around 1915 and worked as an electrical supervisor at the Pennsylvania Dixie Cement Plant. He was a charter member of the First Presbyterian Church when it was organized in March 1917 and served as a deacon and elder for many years. He was also a charter member of the Masonic Lodge 688 F & AM. Prior to his death, he was made a life member. He was survived by his wife, Daisy M. Wright, and two children, Mrs. Malcom Aitken and F.S. Wright. Funeral services were conducted at First Presbyterian Church with the internment following at the City Cemetery.

April 21, 1929

Sparks Circus Clears Out

The Sparks Circus cleared out of town this morning and was headed to its next destination. Early morning signs that the circus was here were the various stands used for the crowds and the tracks in the fields. The paper reported that the Sparks Circus presented a clean, old-fashioned and high-class show for Kingsport. The business district was full of crowds anxiously awaiting to see the circus. Some of the most popular attractions were the animal and acrobatic acts. From Kingsport, the circus made its way to Bluefield, West Virginia.

April 22, 1939

Highway 11-W Association

The newly formed U.S. Highway 11-W Association met on this day at the Kingsport Inn. The organization was formed as a collaborative effort between towns and communities along the highway to secure more tourist traffic. The board of directors was chosen from representatives of twelve communities: Kingsport, Bristol, Blountville, Lee Springs, Surgoinsville, Church Hill, Mooresburg, Pressman's Home, Blain, Rogersville, Bean Station and Rutledge. Officers selected at the meeting include B.F. Warner, manager of the Kingsport Inn (president); B.L. Day, of Pressman's Home (vice-president); and Clifford E. Sanders (secretary/treasurer). The meeting was held at 8:00 p.m. and anyone interested in increasing tourism in the area was invited to attend.

April 23, 1935

Formal Opening of Freels

Freels Drug Store held its formal opening on this day. Headed by Dr. Victor Boyd Freels, the new drugstore opening was expected to draw thousands of people. Dr. Freels came to Kingsport in 1917 and was associated with the Clinchfield Drug Company for many years. The doctor announced in his invitation to the public that special values were to be offered to customers, and "kiddies would be treated to free ice cream cones." The building, located on the corner of Broad and West Center Streets, was erected to house the drugstore on the first floor. Offices and a beauty parlor were located on the second floor, and patrons entered through the side entrance of the building on West Center Street.

April 24, 1926

Trick Golfer

Joe Kirkwood, the world's greatest trick golfer, wowed scores of fans at the Kingsport Country Club. A large crowd was on hand to see Kirkwood perform and hear a lecture on the rudiments of the game. Kirkwood also played in an eighteen-hole foursome match with partner George Penn of Kingsport. Their opponents were Dave Parrish of Bristol and Chut Crimley of Greeneville. Joe Kirkwood was Australia's first international golf superstar. Kirkwood gained great success in his series of stage shows and exhibitions and became well known for his amazing trick shots. One of his most well-known tricks was to rapidly hit two balls, one a hook and the other a slice. Kirkwood was also known for hitting a golf ball from a tee held in the mouth of a woman lying between his feet.

April 25, 1965

Douglass Athletes Honored

On this day, the *Kingsport Times-News* featured a story on the recent annual Douglass High School athletic banquet. The highlight of the annual banquet was the conferring of awards to Douglass High School athletes. An extra award, a humanitarian service award, was presented by the Douglass High School Parent Teacher Association to Charles Lollar. Lollar was recently credited with saving the life of a Kingsport fireman who had suffered heart failure. Ronnie Releford was given a memoriam award in honor of his deceased brother David, who was co-captain of the football team. Patricia Bristol received an award as the captain of the girls' basketball team. Melrose Dobbins and Donald Perry received awards as the male and female athletes with the highest grade-point average. D.A. Henderson, vice-president of Dobyns-Taylor, presented the awards.

April 26, 1937

Car Fire Victims Buried Today

Tennessee Eastman employees Buford Elmo Gray and Carl Porter, both twenty-eight years old, were buried here in Kingsport on this day. The men lost their lives on Saturday night when their car turned over, pinned them underneath and burst into flames. Several people gathered at the scene of the accident, but the intense heat prevented any chance of rescuing the men. The bodies were burned beyond recognition. Porter was identified by a watch and jewelry while Gray was identified by a Tennessee Eastman Corporation (TEC) badge. Gray was a foreman at TEC and a star pitcher on the Eastman City League Baseball team. The accident was being called the most horrible highway tragedy in recent years. Gray's funeral was held at First Methodist Church, where he was a member. He was survived by his parents, Mr. and Mrs. W.H. Gray. Porter's was held at the home of his parents, Mr. and Mrs. L.J. Porter, in Fordtown.

April 27, 1932

The Paste Princess

The Paste Princess closed this evening and was declared a big hit by all. The original musical was produced by the Kingsport Press as a fundraiser for its employee mutual benefit association. The full title of the program was *The Paste Princess, a Musical Comedy in Glue and Paste with More or Less Ink*. The musical was written by press employee William Nordmark and dedicated to E.W. Palmer, president of the Kingsport Press at the time. The play ran for two nights at the Strand Theatre. The characters in the script were based

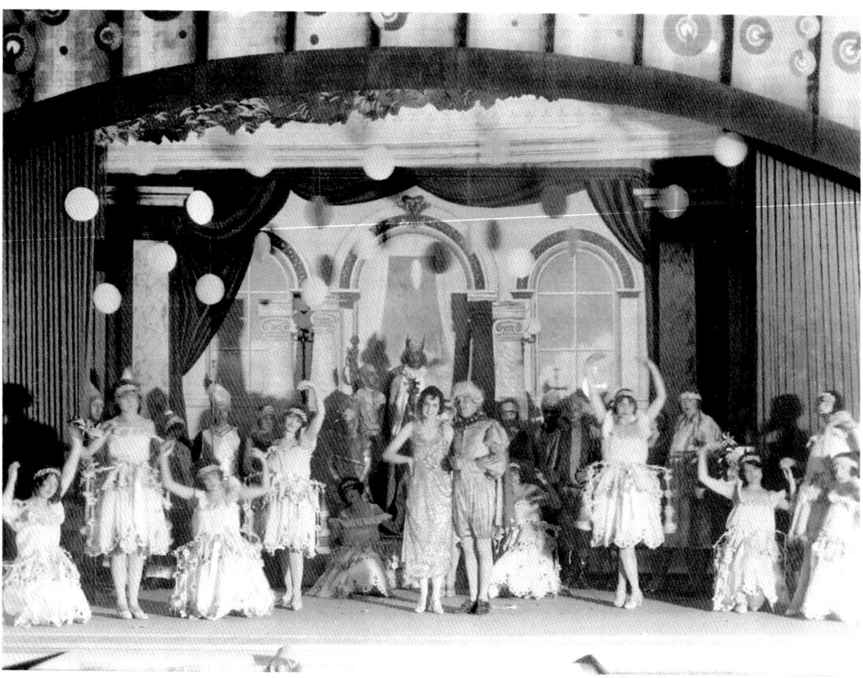

Cast of *The Paste Princess*. *Archives of the City of Kingsport.*

on real people in Kingsport, and the plot included actual occurrences at the press. All of the performers were press employees. Beatrice King Stodola served as art director and acting coach, and the dancers were trained by Larry Doyle.

April 28, 1972

The Man Who Came to Dinner

At 8:00 p.m., Dobyns-Bennett High School Thespian Troupe 432 presented *The Man Who Came to Dinner* by Moss Hart and George Kaufman. The production was directed by Nancy Necessary Pridemore and held at the Little Theater. Charles Petty, Bill McCall and Doug Overby were in charge of staging, and Susan Wescott assisted Nancy Necessary Pridemore. Mrs. Pridemore came to Kingsport to teach English, speech and drama at Dobyns-Bennett High School in 1946 and did so for thirty-nine years, retiring in 1985. The Little Theater at Dobyns-Bennett is named for her. A 1940 graduate of Radford College, the Pridemore Playhouse in Porterfield Hall is also named in her honor. Nancy Necessary Pridemore passed away in April 2003.

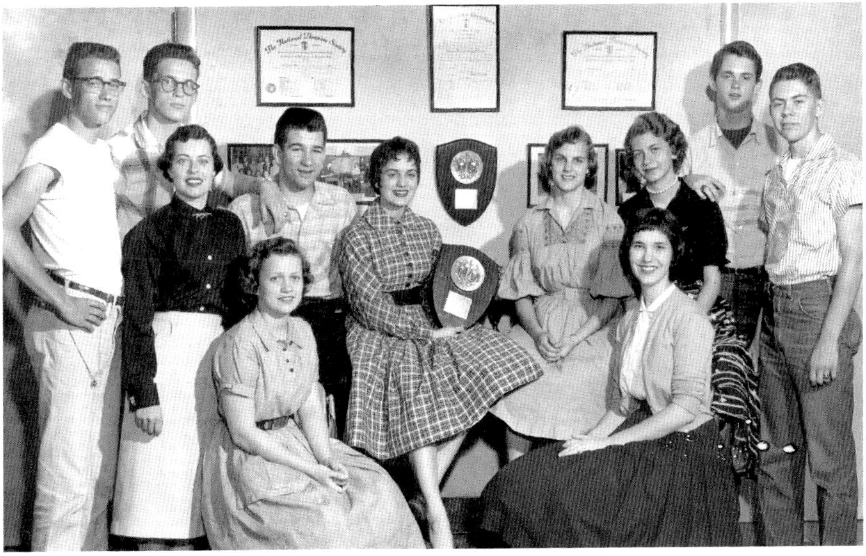

Nancy Pridemore and her theater class. *Archives of the City of Kingsport.*

April 29, 1949

Jankey Utilities and Watson Electric Company Fire

One fireman, Lieutenant Ray Hicks, was killed, and another, John McNew, was admitted to the hospital after a fire swept through buildings on East Market Street. Lieutenant Ray Hicks, who had been with the Kingsport Fire Department since 1942, died of smoke asphyxiation. After less than four years with the fire department, he had been promoted to lieutenant. The buildings that house Jankey Utilities Service Inc. and the Watson Electric Company were almost a total loss; damages from the fire were estimated at nearly $100,000. Apartments were located on the second floor of the building, and at least sixteen people were displaced from their homes due to the fire. The fire was discovered by Bill Arnold of Jankey Utilities around 1:35 p.m. Within minutes, the Kingsport Fire Department arrived, followed shortly by the Kingsport Lifesaving Crew.

April 30, 2011

Daniel Kilgore Signed to 49rs

Kingsport native and Dobyns-Bennett High School graduate Daniel Kilgore was drafted by the San Francisco 49ers on this day in the fifth round of the 2011 NFL Draft. After graduating from Dobyns-Bennett, Kilgore played football at Appalachian State University. As a redshirt freshman at Appalachian State, he recovered a fumble in the end zone for his only career touchdown during the Mountaineers' 49–21 victory over Delaware in the 2007 NCAA Division I Football national championship game. Kilgore earned a bachelor's degree in physical education from Appalachian State University, and he played in Super Bowl XLVII against the Baltimore Ravens. Daniel Kilgore is the son of David and Barbara Kilgore, and he married Megan Tolly, also from Kingsport, in 2015. The couple are supporters of the Tribe Games, a series of Olympic-style events for special-needs youth. The Tribe Games were the brainchild of Jimmy Burleson, a former classmate and teammate of Kilgore's.

MAY

May 1, 1949

Baptismal Drowning

Margaret Chapman, fourteen, drowned in the North Fork of the Holston River during a baptismal ceremony. Franklin Walter Lewis, Chapman's grandfather, had just immersed her when the two lost their footing, and the girl was swept away. A layman, Howard Lee Smith, who was assisting with the baptismal rites, was also swept under the water. Neither he nor Lewis were able to rescue Chapman. The daughter of Mr. and Mrs. Roy Chapman, she was the only one being baptized that afternoon. Her body was found several days after the incident. Lewis and Smith were later arrested and charged with murder, and Mrs. Edna Earl King was charged with aiding and abetting in murder. The charges against all were eventually dropped and the death ruled an accident.

May 2, 1943

Victory Garden Prize Winner

It was announced today that Ross N. Robinson won the first of twelve weekly prizes in the Victory Garden Contest sponsored by twelve Kingsport merchants, the Federation of Garden Clubs and the *Kingsport Times-News*. Robinson's garden was selected over one hundred other Kingsport gardens. The first week's prize was a straw hat, and it was presented to Robinson by Morris Sobel of Sobel's Men's Shop. Robinson's garden tallied nearly a perfect score in the judging. Gardens were judged in six categories: accessibility, plan and arrangement, condition and preparation of the soil, drainage and general impression as a whole. The sixth category was based on the vegetables themselves, and the judges considered vitamins and minerals, foliage condition, quantity, size and variety, rarity, rotation of crops and control of insects and disease.

May 3, 1959

Sassoon Reception

Sir Victor Elias and Lady Sassoon of Nassau, Bahamas, held a reception to celebrate their wedding at the Ridgefields Country Club. Lady Sassoon is the former Maude Evelyn Barnes (Barnsie) of Kingsport. Hosts of

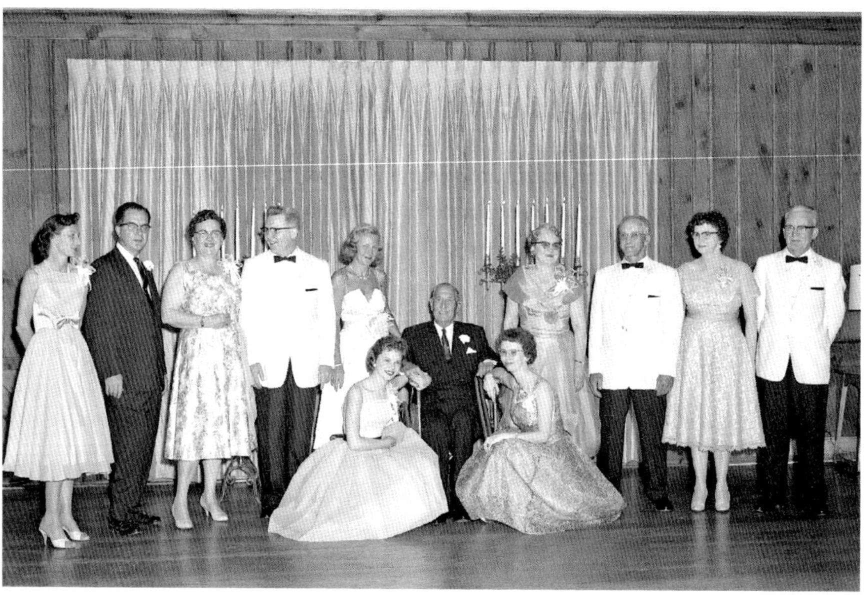

Sir Victor and Lady Sassoon's wedding reception at Ridgefields Country Club. *Archives of the City of Kingsport.*

the reception were Mr. and Mrs. Ernest Barnes, Mr. and Mrs. Bruce Fulkerson, Mr. and Mrs. John Barnes and Mr. and Mrs. James Barnes. Sir Victor Sassoon died a year later, and his widow founded a charity, the Victor Sassoon Heart Foundation. In 2011, the Bahamas Postal Service issued four commemorative postage stamps to highlight the fiftieth anniversary of the Victor Sassoon Heart Foundation.

May 4, 1938

Highland Park Improvement Association

In an announcement made today, highway commissioner J.W. Erwin assured residents of Highland Park that concrete sidewalks would be constructed throughout the suburb within the next few weeks. The announcement, made to the Highland Park Improvement Association, noted that sidewalks would be built on one side of each street and on both sides of Highway 11-W from the city limits to Dickson School. In addition to the sidewalks, the streets will be graded, rocked and ditched for draining purposes. Glenn Kilday, city sanitary inspector, also appeared before the association to speak on a new state statute that would affect residents in Highland Park who raise pigs. The new statute stated that all pigpens must be built outside with wooden floors at least eighteen inches from the ground. Pigs would not be allowed to be kept in garages or stables. Kilday warned residents that they must adhere to the new law.

May 5, 1963

City Hall Dedication

An estimated crowd of nine hundred attended this day's dedication of the newly constructed city hall building on the corner of West Center and Shelby Streets. After music by the Dobyns-Bennett High School band and an invocation by Reverend Leland M. Caulder, the building was presented by Mayor W.W. Cawood and Judge Hal Carr. Judge Jackson C. Raulston gave the featured address for the occasion. After Raulston's address, John Todd Jr. dedicated the building, and Reverend Carroll Skeen gave a benediction. The public was invited to tour the building from 3:00 to 5:00 p.m., and city officials were on hand to greet citizens and answer questions. The building was designed by local architect Allen Dryden, with Armstrong Construction acting as general contractor.

May 6, 1932

"K" Insigne Presented

The Annual "K" Club banquet sponsored by the Parent Teacher Association of Dobyns-Bennett High School was held on this day. A total of eighty-three students received 131 "K" insigne for meritorious work during the past year. Robert Shetterly, one of the outstanding students of the school year, held the record for the largest number of "K's" presented to any one student. Shetterly received 6 for his work in various student activities. Margaret Harrison, George Tipton and William Cigers were each awarded 4. Each student was allowed to bring one guest to the banquet.

May 7, 1917

Federal Dye Stuff and Chemical Company Explosion

Between the hours of 3:00 and 4:00 a.m., an explosion occurred at the Federal Dye Stuff and Chemical Company. According to reports, the explosion was caused by a valve in a pipe that failed to work. Henry Parker was killed instantly, and Paul Logue was fatally injured. Paul Logue had come to Kingsport less than a year before, and he began working as a day laborer for $1.60 a day. At the time of his death, he was a foreman within the company. The explosion and subsequent fire destroyed an entire unit of the plant. At the time of the explosion, production had been running twenty-four hours a day. An investigation was begun to determine if sabotage took place, even though the plant was guarded by federal troops. Federal Dye Stuff and Chemical Company was a short-lived dye-manufacturing plant erected in Kingsport during World War I. The plant was located on all of the one hundred acres of what is now Riverview, plus another one hundred acres east of Riverview, across what is now Wilcox Drive.

MAY 8, 1968

Kingsport Motorist Courtesy Test

The *Kingsport Times-News* conducted a motorist courtesy test involving Joyce Jarvis, nineteen, standing next to her car on Center Street with the hood up, signaling car trouble. First, Joyce dressed like an old lady with glasses on her nose and dress at mid-calf; then, she dressed like a Playboy pinup in a tight dress with miniskirt. Seventy-two cars passed the "old lady" before anyone stopped. The only person to offer help was Neal Gilliam, who was working in his garden nearby and walked over and asked if he could help. After Jarvis let him in on the secret, she went to change clothes. With a shorter skirt, high heels and no glasses, no one went by without stopping for Jarvis in the miniskirt. *Kingsport Times-News* photographer Earl Carter was on the scene to document the motorist courtesy test. Jarvis later worked as a model and director of the Wendy Ward Charm School at Montgomery Ward. The school taught young girls how to paint their nails, walk properly, sit with good posture and conduct themselves like ladies.

MAY 9, 1936

Popeye Club

The first meeting of Popeye Club was held at the State Theater at 10:00 a.m. on this day. The theater's manager, Jimmy Pepper, awarded prizes to those in attendance for the first meeting, and there was a special stage performance by members. Stage settings for the program featured a huge "drop" Popeye sailing into port with the "gang" waiting on the dock to greet him. There was no initiation fee for membership into the club. Children only paid the regular admission price to the theater. This allowed the children to remain for the movie showing after the club meeting.

May 10, 1917

Salvation Army Officers

Captain and Mrs. Leslie Herlan, Salvation Army officers, arrived in Kingsport to take charge of the local Salvation Army. They were here during the absence of Captain and Mrs. A.W. Barbe, who left for Williamson, West Virginia. The Herlens issued a warning to the general public against giving money to beggars on the street. Captain Herlen relayed a very pitiful case appealed to him the other day, but after further investigation it was determined the people were able-bodied but would not work. It was also determined that they were using an accomplice to beg for them.

May 11, 1950

Tennessee Ernie Ford

Legendary entertainer Tennessee Ernie Ford appeared at the State Theater on this day in 1950. Born in Bristol in 1919, Tennessee Ernie Ford was one of the most popular and beloved entertainers of the era, especially in the Tri-Cities region. Ford was a Grand Ole Opry performer, a top recording artist and star of western musical movies. He appeared in Kingsport with his Big Western Show with a "mule train" of musical thrills. Ford performed a matinee and an evening performance. The matinee admission was nine cents for children and forty-eight cents for adults. The price for the evening show was twenty-four cents for children and sixty cents for adults.

May 12, 1924

Tea at Riverview Hospital

The Holston Committee of the Civic League hosted a tea for citizens of Kingsport at the newly finished Riverview Hospital. Mrs. J.W. Lee, chairman of the committee hosting the tea, also noted that the tea was scheduled to coincide with National Hospital Day and would celebrate the opening of the newly furnished hospital. Anyone wishing to attend the tea was provided with free transportation to the hospital through the ladies in charge of the matter through various church organizations. Eleven of the rooms at the hospital were furnished by eleven different organizations within the city. The participating organizations were the Sewing Club, the Presbyterian Auxiliary, the American Legion Auxiliary, the Baraca Class, the Christian Church, the Lutheran Church, the Virginia Club, the Southern Methodist Church, the Northern Methodist Church, the Episcopal Church and the Kingsport Book Club. Guests attending were received by the wives of the hospital directors: Mrs. Felix Geunther, Mrs. Howard Wilson, Mrs. Art Miller, Mrs. S.C. Minnich, Mrs. Guy Pitts and Mrs. E.B. Harris.

May 13, 1985

Spring Revue

Holloway Dance School presented their Spring Revue at 7:30 p.m. this evening at the Ross Robinson Auditorium. The program was presented under the direction and choreography of Reese Holloway Toohey. Accompanists for the program were Wilma Pace and Sandra Stafford. The teaching staff for the Spring Revue included Kathy Cahow, Melinda Leonard, Christy Jinks Albright, Kimberley Perry, Suzie Montgomery and Margaret King. Costumes were directed by Ruth McAmis and Eleanor Ward, and lighting was handled by E.L. Pace. The stage manager for the production was J.E. Toohey. Reese Holloway Toohey, former owner of the Holloway Dance Studio, was the originator of the Christmastime *Nutcracker* performances in Kingsport. She was also one-time director of the Inter City Ballet Company. Toohey, along with her sister, Wilma Pace, a trained pianist, were influential in bringing classical ballet to the Tri-Cities region.

May 14, 1940

Graduates' Day

The Kingsport Merchants Association hosted the first Graduates' Day celebration today. Graduates' Day was organized as a celebration for graduating seniors from Kingsport and the surrounding areas. The program, held at various locations around the city, included a full day of festivities, food and prizes. One of the prizes awarded was a free trip to the New York World's Fair. Graduates from Sullivan, Hawkins, Washington and Greene Counties attended, as well as graduates from Scott and Wise Counties in Virginia. Over one thousand graduates from thirty-nine schools attended the celebration. Flem Dobyns served as chairman for the event. E.W. Palmer, president of the Kingsport Press, delivered the principal address, "American Youth and Citizenship," to the attendees.

May 15, 1945

Scrap Paper Collection

Lewis Hall, president of the Dobyns-Bennett High School Hi-Y Club, reported that 4,800 pounds of scrap paper were collected during the first day's collection of the club's new salvage drive. Hi-Y members formed six teams that canvassed town through the rest of the week and into the next. They collected all salvageable paper to send to the Sullivan County Salvage Committee. The club planned to use any money received from the sale of the material to purchase a war bond for the Dobyns-Bennett High School war memorial fund.

May 16, 1932

The Press Versus Eastman

The Kingsport Press and Eastman Industrial League baseball teams played this evening in an effort to finish the game started several days before that ended in a 4–4 deadlock after six innings of play. The game took place at Edgewood Fields. Ed Dixon's Bookmakers were in second place in the league. A win over the Eastman Chemists would put them in a tie with the Borden Mill Weavers. Professor Thompson of the press led the industrial league with the highest number of hits and the highest batting average. Seaver of the press was close behind.

May 17, 1935

Mrs. Leighton's Piano Recital

Hazel Leighton presented her pupils in a piano recital held on this day. The recital was held at 8:00 p.m. at the Kingsport Utilities Building. The recital, in two parts, featured the following students: Grace Thomas Broyles, Maryana Smith, Ruth Bachelder Fish, Helen McConnell, Robert Cross, Mary Ellen Bradley, Kenneth Hultin, Ruth Hutchins, Grace Jean Lyons, Ernesteene Huskey and Joan Cox. Mrs. Leighton was a well-known music teacher for many years in Kingsport.

May 18, 1936

Kingsport Male Chorus Club

The Kingsport Male Chorus Club made its first public performance debut this evening at the State Theater. The chorus club, organized earlier in the year, had grown rapidly. The club started with a few members and held meetings in the hall of the Methodist church. As interest and membership grew, the club moved meetings to the Kingsport Country Club. Professor DeWitt Miller, assisted by his wife, Mrs. Louise Finley Miller, had coached the chorus since its inception. The chorus club was not necessarily for finished or accomplished singers but rather for those with a keen interest in singing and desire to improve their vocal ability. The Kingsport Male Chorus Club comprised over thirty members.

May 19, 1948

Club 81

The Grand Opening of Club 81, Kingsport's modern nightclub, happened on this day. The chartered club operated exclusively for members, who had to be approved by a five-man executive committee. The club, located on the Greeneville Highway, served dinner from 5:00 to 9:00 p.m. The club specialized in choice cuts of grain-fed beef and seafood in season. The grand opening of the club featured dance music by Sammy DeVault and his orchestra. Closed in December 1949 after a raid by Alcohol Tax Unit agents, it was deemed a public nuisance because liquor was sold and gambling activities occurred.

May 20, 1975

Mary Cunningham

Mary Cunningham was elected to the Kingsport Board of Mayor and Aldermen on this day in 1975. Her election marks the first time a woman had been elected to the BMA in Kingsport. Cunningham was born in Rochester, New York, and is a graduate of Mount Holyoke College with a degree in chemistry. She worked at an atomic power laboratory and for the Harvard School of Public Health before coming to Kingsport. March 3, 2016, was declared "Mary Cunningham Day" by Mayor John Clark.

May 21, 1920

Kingsport Man Killed at Matewan

The *Kingsport Times* reported today that one of the seven Baldwin-Felts detectives killed by miners at Matewan, West Virginia, was A.J. Booher of Kingsport. His family resided on Dale Street. A daughter, Nannie Booher, was a stenographer for the Kingsport Improvement Company. The Booher family had lived in Kingsport for the last six years. Prior to that, they lived in Bristol, where Booher was a police officer for several years. In Kingsport, he was employed as a guard at the Union Dye and Chemical Corporation before leaving to join the Baldwin-Felts organization. The tragedy at Matewan stemmed from the Baldwin-Felts detectives having to evict families of strikers from their homes. A gun battle ensued at the train station between strikers and members of the community. All seven of the detectives were killed. J.A. Powell, a former Bristol police officer, was among the detectives killed.

May 22, 1947

Class Day

The Dobyns-Bennett High School senior class launched its Annual Class Day Program. Using the motif of the sea, skipper (class president) Marvin Goodman acted as master of ceremonies. The ship's log (class history) was read by Carolyn Hoge and sealed orders (class will) were disclosed by Tom Nave. Barbara Gammon read the disaster bill (class prophecy). The class gift, a sum of money to be used for a new speaker stand for the school's auditorium, was presented to Principal K.E. Potts by Goodman.

May 23, 1932

Call of the Banshees

The junior class of Dobyns-Bennett High School presented a mystery play titled *Call of the Banshees*. The play, held in the Dobyns-Bennett High School Auditorium, "promise[d] to be the most thrilling production ever presented on the high school stage." The plot of the play was set in motion by murder, surrounded by superstition and the supernatural and complicated by love interests. The cast included Paul Murrell, Christine Taylor, Howard Wilson, Barnett Haney, Domer Ridings, Kathleen Hutchins, Elaine Neufer, Beverly Burbage, Hollis Cross, William Highsmith, Nancy Stone, Georgia Rowland, Frank Taylor and Faustine White.

May 24, 1971

Bays Mountain Nature Interpretative Center Dedicated

Around four hundred visitors, park officials and dignitaries were present for the opening of the Bays Mountain Nature Interpretative Center. Governor Winfield Dunn was on hand as the principal speaker for the occasion. In a three-part "Act of Acceptance," Kingsport mayor Fred Gillette accepted the center for the community, former mayor Joseph Lewis accepted for industry and Richard Poe, 1970–1971 Teen of the Year, accepted for education. Mayor Lewis was acting in place of James C. White, former board chairman of Tennessee Eastman, who was unable to attend the ceremony. At the time of the dedication, a staff of eight were already on board, as the park had already been opened to visitors on a limited basis in 1968.

May 25, 1929

Prisoner Missing

Charley Grubb, charged with forgery, attended his trial before Judge Campbell but managed to slip out of the courtroom before his sentence was delivered. The incident occurred when the jury went into deliberation. The deliberation lasted only a few minutes, and the jury returned with a verdict of guilty. Judge Campbell summoned for Grubb to appear before him to be sentenced, but Grubb did not appear. A careful search of the courtroom concluded that the prisoner was missing. Grubb evidently walked out of the courtroom and made his getaway before anyone noticed. Judge Campbell failed to pass sentence, as the prisoner was not present to receive it.

May 26, 1929

Montgomery Ward Building

Excavation work on the Montgomery Ward Building on Broad Street was finished, and workmen were preparing the area for concrete work. Once work was completed on the concrete basement, the brick work commenced. The building was constructed adjacent to the First National Bank of Kingsport by Pyle Brothers for J.W. Harrison, former mayor and Kingsport businessman. The building was designed by Allen Dryden with assistance from an architect from the Montgomery Ward Company. A hot air–heating system was installed for the winter, as well as electric fans for the summer. The building was the first in Kingsport to incorporate this hot and cool system. W.J. Heister, a local interior decorator, performed the interior painting and decoration, and the formal opening of Montgomery Ward was held in October 1929.

MAY 27, 1933

Mrs. C.M. Frazier's Accident

Dr. W.H. Reed, attending physician at Kingsport General Hospital, gave an update on the condition of Mrs. C.M. Frazier this evening. Frazier, who was accidentally shot by her six-year-old son, Robert, was reportedly "holding her own." Mrs. Frazier was shot as she was lying on a lounger with her nine-month-old baby. Eight square inches of her skull were blown away by the charge of a shot from a twelve-gauge shotgun, and a portion of her arm was torn by the shot. The gun was accidently discharged by her son, who had climbed up on a piece a furniture in order to play with the gun that was hanging on the wall. Frazier underwent an operation to remove bone fragments from her brain, but it was not believed that the brain was penetrated by the shot itself. During the surgery, a portion of skin was grafted over the wound. According to Dr. Reed, her chances of recovery were fairly good in spite of the seriousness of her injury.

MAY 28, 1933

Baccalaureate Services

Baccalaureate services were held this evening at Dobyns-Bennett High School. The 1933 graduating class was one of the largest in recent years, with a total of sixty-five students—twenty-eight boys and thirty-seven girls. The program opened with a prelude by the Dobyns-Bennett High School orchestra, followed by the processional. Reverend J.L. Trent of Calvary Baptist delivered the sermon, a special address for the students who would now be earning a living or continuing their education.

MAY 29, 1936

Highland Park Fire

William "Bill" Lee Hatcher was killed in Highland Park when flames ravaged through the area on this day. The buildings destroyed include the Hutch-

Wallin Floral Shop, Barger Distribution Company, Pastime Tavern and the Moseley residence. The fire was said to have started in the rear room of the building where two girls, employees of the Pastime Tavern, resided. The origin of the fire is not known. All of the occupants of the building, except Hatcher, were able to escape unharmed. The fire raged for several hours while firefighters attempted to keep it from spreading. Several firemen were slightly injured in the blaze. Dr. Will Hutchins, owner of the building, had about $2,000 coverage. Mr. George Barger, of the Barger Distribution Company, said there was no insurance on the tavern or the distribution company.

May 30, 1942

Legion Pool

The Legion Pool opened for the first day of the summer season to a record crowd. Around six hundred flocked to the pool for opening day, making it the largest crowd in the last three years. The first person to officially hit the pool on this day was Jay Fleener. The first swimmers of the season were two young boys who snuck into the pool the night before. Their preseason swim was cut short by the spotlight of a police cruiser. The boys were said to have fled the scene sans clothes but later retrieved them. This year, the city had plans to not keep the pool open late enough to use the lights. The government granted permission for the city to obtain the chemicals needed to maintain the pool but asked that efforts be made to conserve electric power. The pool closed before complete darkness.

May 31, 1949

Camp Sky-Wa-Mo

"If we had known you were coming, we'd a baked a cake." That was the theme of the Bristol and Kingsport Girl Scouts on their first camping trip to Camp Sky-Wa-Mo. In total, there were thirty-five campers from Bristol and

Kingsport. The girls hiked, cooked outdoors, sang, held a talent show, played games and made a lot of memories and friends. The Kingsport Scouts from Troop 45 included Carol Ann Kelley, Mary Clemmer, Jeanette Carmichael, Lynn Faw, Mary Lee Gift, Suzanne Gannaway, Jean Lee Watkins, Delores Ginn, Patty Hurt, Elaine Ellenberg, Catharine Pollard, Sandra Poole, Janice Johnson, Beverly McIntyre, Sarah Hetherington, Patricia McCollum and Marilyn Faulk. Troop leaders Mrs. Wendell Faw, Mrs. Edgar Gift and Mrs. Fred Watkins accompanied the campers.

JUNE

June 1, 1938

Legion Pool Activities

The American Legion pool reported that it would be hosting a number of new and fun events at the pool throughout the summer. Howard Hale, swimming instructor, announced that special courses in swimming for children would take place at the American Legion Pool. The courses would include classes for beginners and instruction in diving. Hale was also taking registration for adult lifesaving courses. Classes were held each day at the pool. Legion Pool Park officials also announced that they planned to present a number of water pageants. The pool and recreation center also hosted a recreational hour from 11:00 a.m. to 12:00 p.m., when swimmers would be divided according to age to participate in games and contests.

June 2, 1950

Charles Store

The Charles Store, on the corner of Broad and Market Streets, originally opened in April 1929. Having recently completed a significant and third expansion, the store celebrated its grand reopening on this day. One of the biggest changes was the addition of a marble clock tower on the façade. The festivities featured a helicopter that released a balloon shower to the crowd below. Dr. E.W. Tipton, owner of the Charles Building, cut the ribbon during the opening ceremonies. In addition to modernizing the building, a new floor was added. The entire store was air conditioned, and new fluorescent lighting was installed. The new store featured two large murals depicting Kingsport and its industries.

June 3, 1968

Suicidal Woman

Tennessee Valley Authority guard H.E. Garland was on duty at the overlook station at Fort Patrick Henry Dam when a woman asked permission to use the phone. As he was leaving the station to give the woman privacy, Garland overheard the woman tell the other person on the line that she was going to end it all by jumping off the dam. Garland was able to detain the woman, who made several unsuccessful attempts to take his gun. The Kingsport Police Department was called, and patrolman H.E. McConnell arrived at the scene shortly. McConnell was forced to handcuff the woman in order to transport her to the police station, where a minister was waiting.

June 4, 1948

Dance Recital

Charles Ryburn presented his School of Dance in a recital this evening. The recital, held in the junior high school auditorium, featured Mack Ray Jr. as master of ceremonies. The first scene of the recital, *Café Society*, featured the youngest children in the school. The Charles Ryburn dance studio was located at 102 West Park, at the corner of Broad Street. Ryburn opened his dancing school in 1941. Registration for the very first classes was held at the Homestead Hotel, and anyone aged four to forty was encouraged to register for classes. Charles Ryburn was born on March 8, 1913, in Erwin,

Tennessee. He owned the Charles Ryburn School of Dance for almost fifty years, retiring from teaching at the age of eighty-one. He passed away in 2012, one day after celebrating his ninety-ninth birthday.

June 5, 1936

Rotherwood Bridge Collapse

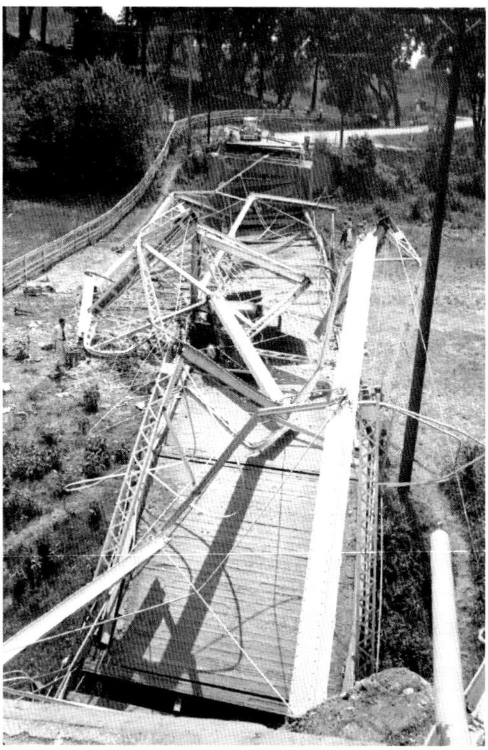

Rotherwood Bridge collapse. *Archives of the City of Kingsport.*

Five people narrowly escaped death when the Rotherwood Bridge collapsed. The bridge, which linked Sullivan and Hawkins Counties, collapsed around 11:00 p.m. E.O. Trent, a truck driver for L and C Fruit Company, was en route to Kingsport when the bridge collapsed. Trent's truck fell with the bridge and was buried in the rubble. Trent suffered only a cut on his head. Witnesses described his escape from death as miraculous. Another car, with four people traveling to Rogersville, stopped just as it was about to plunge off the bridge. Damage from the collapse was estimated at about $10,000. Traffic was rerouted over a nine-mile detour via Weber City, on the Gate City Highway, through Holston Springs and down the North Fork of the Holston River. The bridge was erected around 1913. For some time, efforts had been underway to obtain a new bridge, but the matter had always been deferred.

June 6, 1976

Donelson Flatboat Reenactment

On this day, as part of America's bicentennial celebrations, three flatboats (*Adventure II*, *Rachel* and *Charlotte*) were constructed and used to replicate the John Donelson voyage. The Donelson family, along with thirty other families, embarked from Fort Patrick Henry Dam in December 1779. By April 1780, they reached Big Salt Lick (now Nashville). The reenactment voyage left Netherland Inn in Kingsport on June 6, 1976, and arrived in Nashville on August 7, 1976. The reenactment followed all 1,006 miles of the original voyage. Following the reenactment, the flatboat *Charlotte* was returned to the Netherland Inn, and it is still on display as of this writing.

June 7, 1919

Women Voters

This day marked the first time in history that women were allowed to vote in Kingsport's municipal election. Citizens were voting on the selection of the BMA as well as on an issue involving funding for three new schools in Kingsport. Women represented roughly 15 percent of the 750 registered voters in Kingsport.

June 8, 1966

Douglass High School Closed

The doors on Douglass High School officially closed on this day. Nineteen Douglass High School seniors graduated at the thirty-fifth and final commencement of the school. Students at Douglass who had not yet graduated were assimilated into the city's white schools. At the time of its closing, Douglass High School was the largest African American school in northeastern Tennessee, southwestern Virginia and southeastern Kentucky. Douglass High School, which included elementary and junior

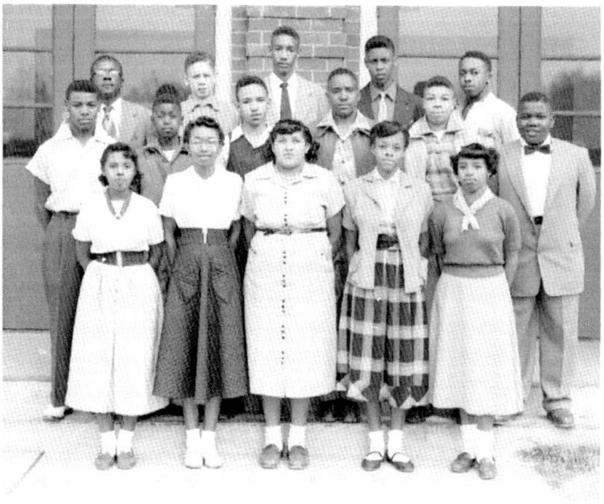

Douglas High School class portrait, 1953. *Archives of the City of Kingsport.*

high schools as well, was originally called the Oklahoma Grove School, begun in 1913 when the all-white Kingsport Public School moved to a new building and location, and its old building became the school for black children. In 1928, a new school, partially funded by the Rosenwald Foundation, was built. By 1951, Douglass had moved into a new building in the Riverview Community.

June 9, 1935

Tranbarger Produce Company Break-In

Merchant policeman Raymond Morse thwarted a break-in at the R.B. Tranbarger Produce Company on Market Street. While making his rounds, Officer Morse came upon the would-be intruder as he attempted to break into the rear door of the store. Officer Morse chased the burglar for several blocks, but the burglar escaped into the swamps of the Blackbottom section of town. The thief, in his haste to get away, left some of his clothing at the store, where he apparently had laid them as he attempted to pry the lock.

June 10, 1951

George Washington Carver Library

The first public library branch of the Kingsport Public Library system held its grand opening and dedication today. The George Washington Carver Library on Douglass Street was designed by local architect Allen N. Dryden Sr. The name of the library was chosen from a contest conducted by the students at Douglass School. Representatives from the Housing Authority Board, BMA, Board of Education and Board of Trustees of the Kingsport Library participated on the program. Colonel E.W. Palmer represented the Kingsport Public Library Board. Also included on the program were the Negro Community Chorus and Mrs. H.T. Stacy, an active Citizens Library Movement member. The George Washington Carver Library closed in October 2007.

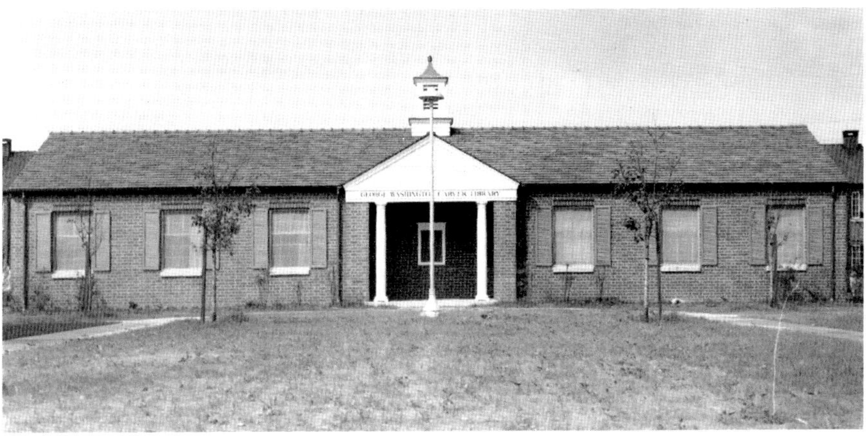

George Washington Carver Library in Riverview. *Archives of the City of Kingsport.*

June 11, 1953

Curved Bars Awarded

Nine Curved Bars were presented to members of Troop 45. The Curved Bar was the highest award in Girl Scouting from 1940 to 1963 and given for earning sixteen badges. The award ceremony was held at the Mafair Methodist Church, and Mrs. Duncan, Girl Scout council president, presented

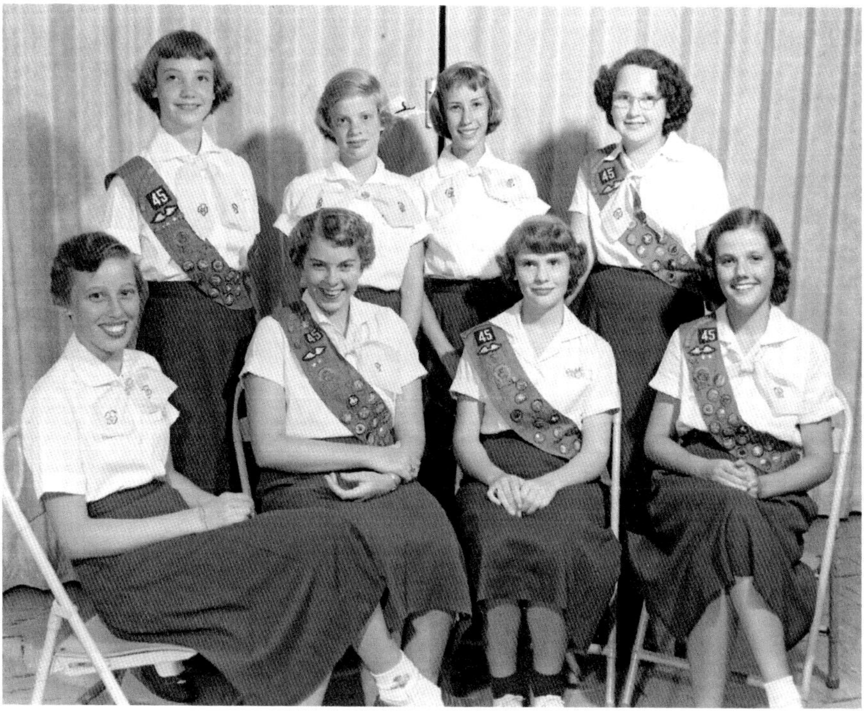

Portrait of Girl Scout Troop 45, 1953. *Archives of the City of Kingsport.*

the Curved Bars to Mary Lee Gift, Elaine Ellenburg, Carol Ann Kelly, Ann Pollard, Beverly McIntyre, Lynn Faw, Pat McCullum, Jeanette Carmichael and Jean Lee Watkins. Mrs. Wendell Faw was their troop leader.

June 12, 1937

Legion Pool Opens

Although open since May 29, 1937, the Legion Pool was officially dedicated on this day by Governor Gordon Browning and Senator George L. Berry. A crowd of ten thousand was anticipated for the opening. The pool was owned and operated by members of the American Legion Hammond Post No. 3. The land was purchased in 1936 to construct a recreation center, with the swimming pool being the first project. The total cost of the land and construction of the pool was $53,000, and a year after the pool opened, the

American Legion donated the pool and the land to the City of Kingsport. In May 1975, the city held a grand reopening of the Legion Pool that featured a new configuration to the pool that was constructed by Armstrong Construction and designed by architect Charles M. Graves of Atlanta. The Legion Pool closed in 2012. The pool property, including buildings, was demolished shortly thereafter.

June 13, 1983

Gerald Sensabaugh

On this day in 1983, Gerald L. Sensabaugh Jr. was born. Sensabaugh is a former professional football player from Kingsport. He was drafted by the Jacksonville Jaguars in the fifth round of the 2005 NFL Draft. A graduate of Dobyns-Bennett High School, Sensabaugh played college football at East Tennessee State University until the college disbanded its football program. Sensabaugh transferred to the University of North Carolina and played for the Tar Heels for one season. Sensabaugh's forty-six-inch vertical leap at the 2005 NFL Combine set a new record for the highest vertical leap—a record that still stands today. In 2009, he was signed by the Dallas Cowboys. Sensabaugh retired from the NFL in 2013. He has chosen to pursue a career in professional bass fishing.

June 14, 1950

Milk Ordinance

The BMA passed, on the third reading, an amendment to the Milk Ordinance that would allow the sale of milk pasteurized outside of Sullivan County here in Kingsport. Formerly, the ordinance required that milk sold in Kingsport be pasteurized in Sullivan County. City attorney H. Marvin Parsons argued that the section in the ordinance violated constitutional free trade rights. Eugene Hunter, attorney for Southern Maid, said the amendment would not affect the power of city health officers to control the finished product. They would still be allowed to inspect all milk products brought to Kingsport for sale.

June 15, 1950

Ex-Kingsport Spy Arrested

Alfred Dean Slack was arrested at his home in Syracuse, New York, on espionage charges stemming from his time working in Kingsport at Holston Ordnance Works between 1943 and 1944. Slack had worked with fellow spy Harry Gold, and Slack provided him with information on the explosive RDX, manufactured as "Compound B," that was used in World War II and more powerful than TNT. Slack was extradited to Tennessee, where he stood trial in Greeneville. Slack was sentenced to fifteen years in prison.

June 16, 1937

Arroway Factory

Officials of the Arroway Traffic Signal Corporation announced on this day that a plant for the manufacture of the company's product will be built in Kingsport. The plant was to be located in Highland Park on property owned by Dr. Will Hutchins. The Arroway Traffic Signal Corporation was a Kingsport Company that was organized about two years earlier. The majority of the stockholders were residents of the city. Arroway offices were located in the Kingsport Industrial Bank Building. A branch office had been opened in Detroit, Michigan, where the signals were manufactured until a plant could be built in Kingsport. The Arroway light was invented by R.O. Ferguson of Bristol. In June 1938, the first Arroway traffic signal was placed in Kingsport, at the corner of Market and Cherokee Streets. In 1939, Arroway filed an involuntary petition for bankruptcy.

June 17, 1971

Guilty

D.S. Stapleton of Lynn Garden waived a jury trial and pled guilty to manslaughter. He was sentenced by Judge Conway Smith to eleven months and twenty-nine days in jail after hearing testimony from the Sheriff Bill Nelms. Stapleton was charged with the murder of Miller Gardener at a house he rented on the Hawkins-Sullivan County line. Gardener died from a single gunshot to the head. The shooting stemmed from a disagreement over cards. Gardener, a known fighter, grabbed Stapleton by the hair and tried to start a fight with him. Stapleton proceeded to pull his gun and shoot Gardner.

June 18, 1952

Dr. Smith and Wife Found Dead

An ambulance, carrying the bodies of Dr. S.L. Smith and Mrs. Smith, was en route to Kingsport on this day from Orangeburg, South Carolina. The couple had been found dead in their Orangeburg Hotel Room by a maid who opened the door of the room after receiving no response from knocking on the door or from phoning the room. Dr. and Mrs. Smith had slashes to both of their left wrists, and both had their throats cut through the jugular vein. Officers had yet to determine how the couple died but stated that it was a case of "murder-suicide" or "double suicide." The room had no evidence of a break-in, as it was locked from the inside, and no money or valuables appeared to be taken. Dr. Smith was sixty-six years old, his wife forty-three. Their marriage was the second for both, and both had children from their previous marriages.

June 19, 1957

Speeding Ticket

A man showed up to city court on this morning to pay the fine on a speeding ticket. Of course, that in itself isn't that unusual or anything of note. The story behind it, however, is pretty amusing. Patrolman Paul Porter and Albert Fletcher stopped a man for speeding. The officers relayed that the man asked, "Fellows, can't we do something about this without going to court?" The officers first thought the man was trying to bribe them, but he explained that a few days earlier his wife had gotten a ticket and he had

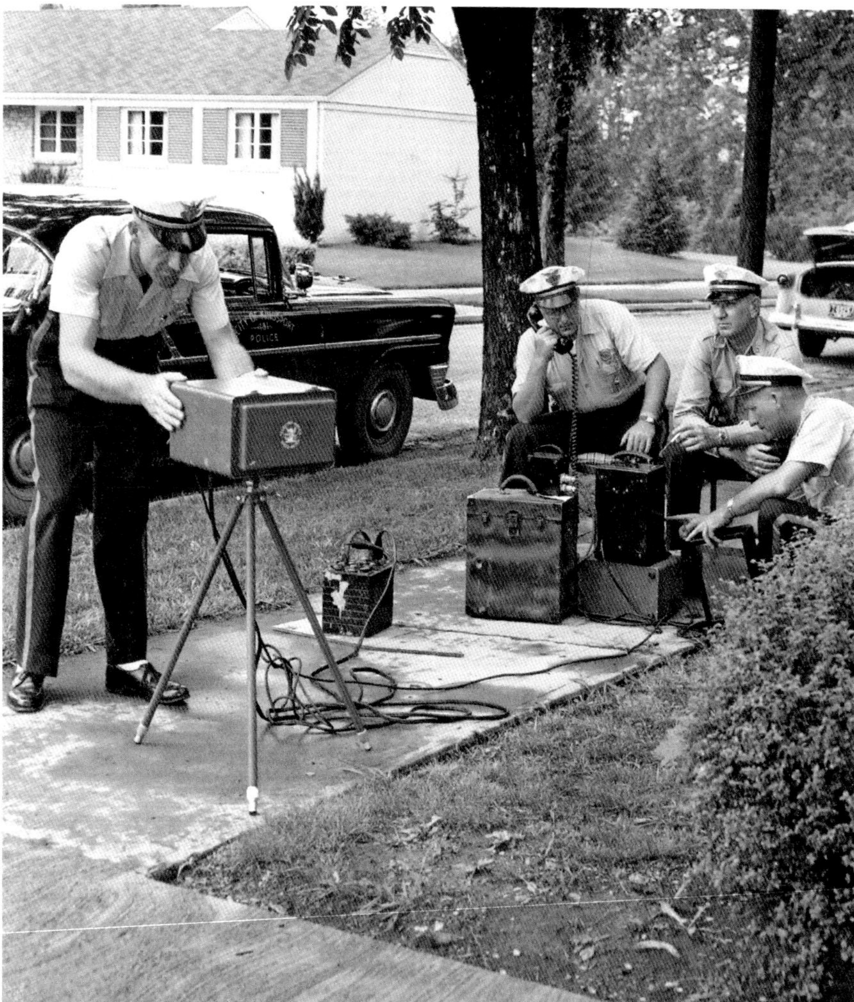

Kingsport Police Department demonstrating radar, June 1957. *Archives of the City of Kingsport.*

raised holy hell with her. The man proclaimed, "I really gave her a riding. If you give me a ticket, I'll never hear the last of it." The officers, both married, were sympathetic, but the man showed up anyway to pay his fourteen-dollar fine. His wife was there, beaming brightly.

June 20, 1966

Road Closed

The west side of Broad Street between Sullivan and Main Streets was closed to traffic on this day. Traffic lanes and parking lanes were painted and repaired throughout the day by the Kingsport Public Works Department. Two-way traffic moved into the two lanes on the east side of the normally four-lane street. The Safety Department planned to repaint angle parking lanes while the Public Works Department made some minor asphalt repairs. The landscape of Broad Street has seen many changes throughout Kingsport's history. Originally, it was designed with parkways and medians, but they were removed in the late 1930s. The project increased the traffic lanes, extended the sidewalks and allowed for angle parking on the street. Today, Broad Street features smaller traffic lanes with angle parking in the middle of the street.

June 21, 1957

Miss Kingsport and Miss Sullivan County

The winners of the Miss Sullivan County and Miss Kingsport pageants were decided at the end of the pageant this evening. In front of a crowd of two

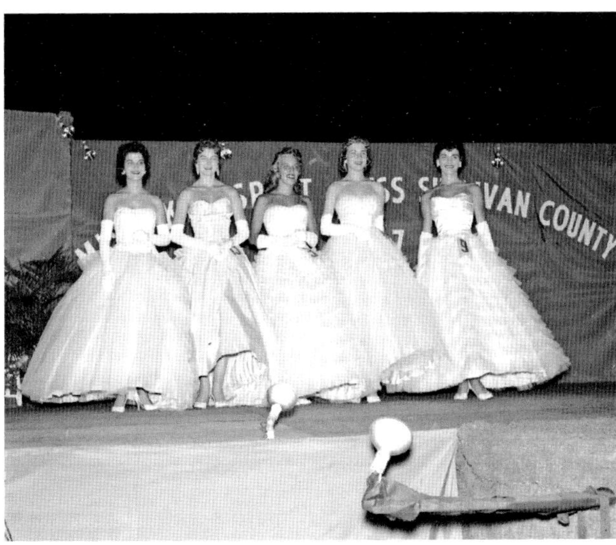

Miss Kingsport/ Miss Sullivan County Pageant contestants, 1957. *Archives of the City of Kingsport.*

thousand, Jeanette Conkin was crowned Miss Sullivan County, and Louise Slaughter was crowned Miss Kingsport. Both Conkin and Slaughter will go on to the Miss Tennessee Pageant. Slaughter is a 1957 graduate of Dobyns-Bennett High School. She played the piano for her talent exhibition. She is the daughter of Mr. and Mrs. Paul Slaughter of Valley Street. Conkin is a graduate of Sullivan High School and works as an airline stewardess. For her talent exhibition, she pantomimed to Betty Hutton's recording of "Stuff Like That There" She is the daughter of Mr. and Mrs. Roy Conkin of Sullivan Gardens.

June 22, 1928

Dr. Paul E. Marsh

The funeral for Dr. Paul E. Marsh was held today. Dr. Marsh, a prominent physician and surgeon in Kingsport, died on the operating table after a freak accident in which his wrist was slashed after a fall into his garage window. The doctor, on his way to a call, fell and tried to catch himself, but his hand went through glass, cutting his wrist and severing blood vessels, nerves and tendons. He was taken to the Marsh Clinic, located on Charlemont Street. Dr. O.S. Hauk was summoned and first aid rendered. Realizing the possibility of Marsh's hand being crippled, the injured physician was sent to a surgeon in Knoxville. He died unexpectedly while there. Only thirty-six years old, Dr. Paul Marsh had been operating the Marsh Clinic, a local hospital, for the last few years.

June 23, 1946

Drowning at Silver Lake

George Cifers, twenty-one, died in a heroic rescue attempt at Silver Lake. Cifers, a former World War II sailor, perished while trying to save the life of another youth. The boy that Cifers was attempting to rescue had been caught on an electric wire over the pool. Cifers, in his rescue attempt, got caught up in the wires. Officers were unable to determine if his death was caused by electrocution or drowning. Cifers's drowning prompted one of the largest lawsuits in Kingsport history. The Holston Electric Cooperative was ultimately charged with negligence, and $12,000 in damages was awarded to the plaintiffs.

June 24, 1951

Joe Higgins

Joe Higgins died on this day. Higgins was a leading figure in the history of organized baseball in Kingsport and the Appalachian League. Higgins came to Kingsport from New York in 1923, and he worked as a linotype operator at the Kingsport Press. Joe Higgins was the also the first Santa aboard the Santa Train, a role he played from 1943 to 1950. During that time, he also played Santa around town at various functions for the holidays, including playing Santa at W.B. Greene Company. Joe Higgins took his role as Santa very seriously, even attending Santa School so he could more realistically portray the jolly Kris Kringle.

June 25, 1919

Court Date Set

The *Kingsport Times* announced that the trial regarding the murder of Jasper Bridwell in March had been set for the following Monday. Kingsport policemen S.P. Dickson and W.M. Lee and jitney driver J.H. Morris would be tried for the murder. Bridwell was killed while driving with his father toward the city, just east of the Rotherwood Bridge. The policemen had been told that the young Bridwell would be coming through the city with whiskey. They had Morris, the jitney driver, drive them to the bridge, where they met the Bridwells. In the attempt to stop them, Bridwell pulled out a pistol, so the officers claimed it was self-defense. Bridwell's father maintains the shooting was done without cause. Dickson and Lee were both acquitted on all charges. When the trial was complete, both officers resigned from the police department.

June 26, 1966

Gravely Road Fire

A.P. Wright, the father of Bill Wright, the Republican candidate for sheriff of Sullivan County, was injured while fighting a fire in his home. The blaze at the Wright home on Gravely Road was discovered by a neighbor who saw smoke coming out the window. A.P. Wright suffered serious cuts to his hands and arms as he was breaking out of a bedroom window, and he was treated at Holston Valley Community Hospital. Neighbors attempted to put out the blaze but were unable to do so. The fire department was called and had the blaze out in under ten minutes.

June 27, 1921

Church Accused of Stealing Car

The preliminary hearing of Rufus Church, charged in the theft of a Ford touring car belonging to E.B. Harris, got underway today. Magistrate H.O. Bunn presided over the hearing. The car was allegedly taken from in front of the White House Café on Broad Street. Mr. Harris offered a fifty-dollar reward that was answered by Marvin Clayton, who told Harris where the car was. After further investigation, it was learned that Clayton was with Church when the car was stolen. Clayton was later arrested and faced the same charges as Church.

June 28, 1933

Other Man's Job

The Rotary Club hosted a unique program during its noon luncheon meeting. Five speakers gave five-minute presentations on the proper methods of handling businesses other than their own. H.J. Shivell, manager of Slip-Not Belting Corporation, spoke on what is wrong with the dentistry business; Dr. T.T. McNeer of Marsh Clinic and Hospital talked about issues with the ministerial calling; Dr. Will Hutchins, dentist, described the proper method to operate the Kingsport Press; John B. Nall, realtor, discussed the telephone company; and Dr. T.P. Johnston, pastor at First Presbyterian Church, explained why he gave up medicine to become a minister.

June 29, 1956

World Tour

Ronnie Tittle, an eleven-year-old Kingsport boy, set out to see the world but only made it as far as Bristol. Tittle told police that he wasn't intending to run away and wasn't mad at anyone, he just wanted to look around. Bristol police found him on the Abingdon Highway, just inside the city limits, and returned him to his parents. Tittle walked the entire distance from his home on Bloomingdale Road to where he was picked up by police.

June 30, 1956

General Sessions Court

A Kingsport woman was charged with public profanity, but the case was dismissed by acting Judge Frank Moore, presiding for Judge S.G. Gilbreath. During the same general session court, four men were found guilty of possessing whiskey, two persons were charged with public drunkenness and one man was charged with reckless driving. One case was bound over after he pleaded not guilty to charges of public drunkenness.

JULY

July 1, 2001

Bobby Cifers Dies

Robert Gale "Bobby" Cifers died on this day. A native of Kingsport, Cifers was considered one of the greatest high school athletes from Tennessee. A standout in both football and track and field, at the University of Tennessee he led the football team to victory in the 1943 Sugar Bowl. Cifers played in the NFL for the Detroit Lions, the Pittsburgh Steelers and the Green Bay Packers. Along with his NFL All-Pro brother Ed Cifers, he is part of the only pair of brothers in the Tennessee State Sports Hall of Fame.

July 2, 1957

Midget League Baseball

Playing in front of a crowd of three hundred spectators at J. Fred Johnson Park, the Optimist Club Midget League Baseball team proved why it was the league champion for the first half of the season. The team went up against the Midget League All-Star team and won 20–2. The Optimist

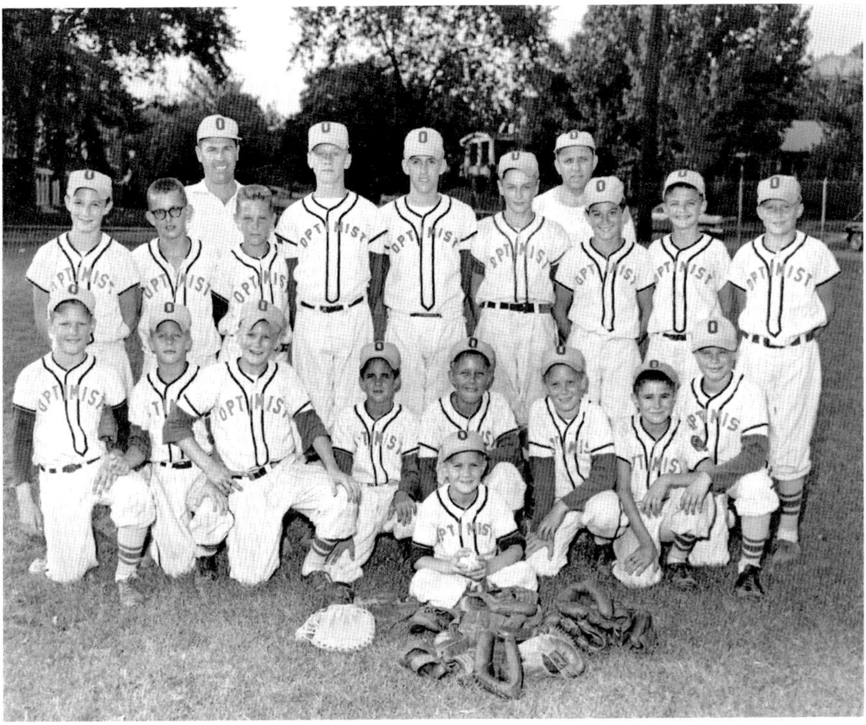

Kingsport City Recreation League, Optimist Club baseball team. *Archives of the City of Kingsport.*

team gave up two runs in the first inning but roared out front with a six-run barrage in the third inning and never looked back. The Rotary Club and Civitan teams were reported to be the only teams that may have a chance of beating this season's Optimist Team.

July 3, 1919

First City Manager Resigns

Kingsport's first city manager, William R. Pouder, resigned his position on this day at a BMA meeting. The resignation would take effect when a successor was found. Pouder came to Kingsport from Johnson City, where he had been city recorder and treasurer. Pouder's resignation was partly attributed to his disagreements with the board and his refusal to make concessions to certain citizens whom he considered against the best interests of the city. Herbert Kidd, assistant city engineer from Knoxville, was chosen as the next city manager. Meanwhile, Pouder took a position as manager of the board of commerce in Knoxville.

July 4, 1919

Life Is Easy

Taking life "easy" was the mantra for this year's Independence Day celebration in Kingsport. Kingsport celebrated the Fourth of July by closing up virtually every shop and factory. The post office, banks and almost every store suspended work for the day. The movies, however, promised big business, as the Strand Theatre broadcasted the Willard-Dempsey fight. It was a great day for people to take motor trips to the country for picnics or attend other Independence Day celebrations.

July 5, 1926

Alvin York Comes to Town

A large crowd of Kingsporters gathered downtown on this day to see Sergeant Alvin C. York, one of the most decorated American soldiers from World War I. The event was organized by the American Legion, Hammond Post. York was introduced to the crowd, estimated at twenty thousand, by J. Fred Johnson. The celebration was the greatest in Kingsport's history at that time. The day was celebrated with a parade, music and speeches. City officials gave York a grand tour of the city, taking him to Cement Hill, local schools and plants and to the Kingsport Press, where he was given a tour by E.W. Palmer.

July 6, 1950

Dixie Study Club

How churches of the South have played a part in history was the topic of discussion by Mrs. R.P. Moss at the meeting of the Dixie Study Club. The club met at the home of Mrs. Will Hutchins. Assisting Mrs. Hutchins in serving refreshments were Mrs. Sullivan and Mrs. D.W. Black. Twenty members in attendance learned about several churches in the South, including the "Old Kingsport" Church that was established in 1826. Mrs. Mack Shipley presided over the meeting, and the "resolve for the year" was read in unison. Mrs. B.B. Sullivan ended the meeting with a prayer. The Dixie Study Club was organized in March 1939 for its members to study southern literature and history. Membership in the club was limited to women from southern states. Charter members of the club included Mrs. J. W. Shuey, Mrs. S.W. Carrell, Mrs. John R. Todd, Mrs. M.W. Gillenwater, Mrs. B.B. Sullivan, Mrs. Joe Riley, Mrs. Eugene Spencer, Miss Bess Stephenson and Miss Ethel Warrick.

July 7, 1919

Illicit Distilling

Tom Dickson was in jail, and his son, Fred, was hiding out somewhere in the mountains with a bullet wound to his arm. These events were all related to

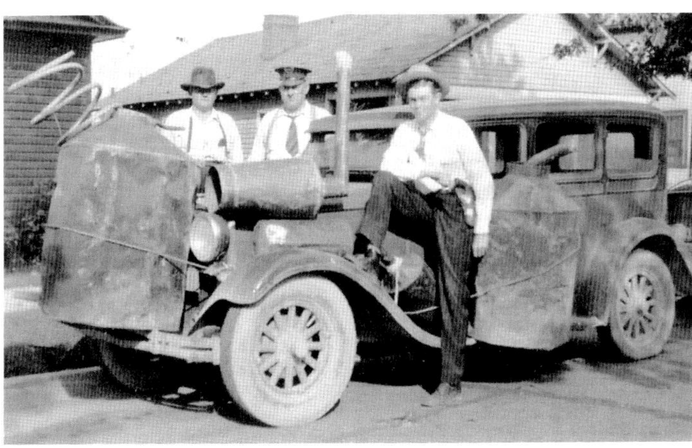

Patrolman Thompson, Chief Robert "Bob" Saylor and Constable Monty Upchurch pose with an illicit moonshine still they seized, circa 1925. *Archives of the City of Kingsport.*

the raid made on this day by Deputy Sheriff W.P. Flora and Sam P. Dickson on a whiskey still in a corncrib on the Dickson property. The officers seized an eighty-gallon copper still and a half gallon of corn whiskey. Dickson admitted the still and whiskey were his and was being held on a charge of illicit distilling. Dickson's son, Fred, ran when he saw the officers. Sheriff Flora fired at him, striking him in the arm.

July 8, 1919

Life and Health Insurance Policies for Kingsport Industries

The *Kingsport Times* announced today that life insurance policies and health insurance policies would be provided for every man and woman employed in Kingsport Industries. The health insurance policies would provide half pay for illnesses, and over one thousand men and women would benefit from these policies. The premiums for the policies were to be paid for by the various industries in the city, including the Kingsport Brick Company, Kingsport Improvement Company, Kingsport Farms, Kingsport Stores Inc., Clinchfield Portland Cement Corporation, Kingsport Extract Corporation, Kingsport Tanneries, Kingsport Utilities, Kingsport Pulp Corporation and Kingsport Hosiery Mills.

July 9, 1948

Meet Mr. Spudnut

An announcement was made on this day that another shop in the rapidly growing system of Spudnut Shops would be opening in Kingsport. The Spudnut, marketed as America's Finest Food Confection, was developed in Salt Lake City by Al and Bob Pelton. In 1946, the brothers began establishing a nationwide chain of franchised Spudnut Shops. By 1948, there were over two hundred Spudnut Shops. The Kingsport shop was located at 1582 Bristol Highway. It was owned and operated by L.M. Parks and was the 209th Spudnut Shop. The opening day of the shop on the Bristol Highway included free spudnuts and coffee for fifteen minutes every hour, on the hour. Spudnuts are made with a special blend of wheat flour, dehydrated potatoes, milk solids, whole fresh eggs and other ingredients.

July 10, 1947

Dobyns-Bennett High School Fire

The Kingsport Fire Department responded to a fire at Dobyns-Bennett High School, but it had already completely destroyed the school's auditorium. Stuart Day, with the Barter Theater Players, narrowly escaped being trapped by the fire. Day was in the men's dressing room getting ready for his role in the play *East Lynne* that was to take place that evening in the auditorium. The Barter Players reported all of their scenery, lighting and costumes were lost in the fire. The fire, which originated backstage, quickly swept through the

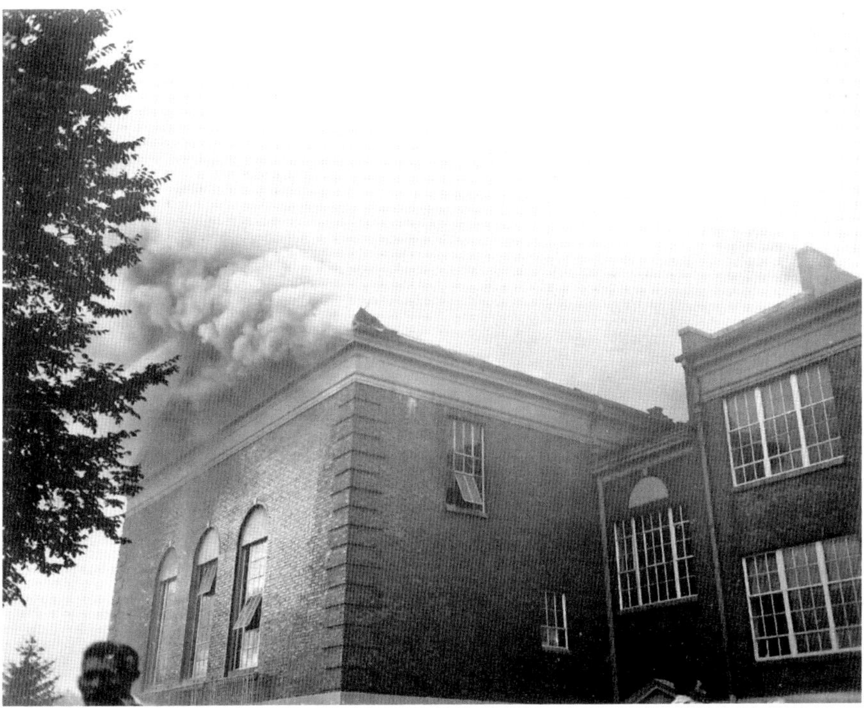

Dobyns-Bennett High School auditorium fire. *Archives of the City of Kingsport.*

auditorium and up to the roof of the building. The fire damage was mostly contained in the auditorium, but the rest of the school suffered damage from smoke and water.

July 11, 1917

Charter for Kingsport Red Cross Granted

In June 1917, a group of Sullivan County citizens came together to organize and request a charter for a Red Cross chapter in Kingsport. The charter for the Kingsport chapter of the Red Cross was granted on this day. J. Fred Johnson was elected chairman, and other officers elected included Mrs. J.W. Dobyns (vice-chairman), A.D. Brockman (treasurer) and Dora W. Stone (secretary). William Roller, R.J. Hazel, William R. Pouder, T.B. Yancey, W.M. Bennett, R.B. Embree, M.B. Cainblos and R.C. Johnson were members at large. Frank Cloud became chapter chairman in 1918 and served in this capacity until 1942.

July 12, 2011

Dedication of Holston Valley Medical Center Heritage Museum

The Holston Valley Medical Center held the dedication of its new Heritage Museum today. The museum chronicles the changes and growth of the hospital and celebrates its history since its opening in 1935. The museum features photographic murals, an extensive timeline of the hospital and medical artifacts. The creation of the museum was spearheaded by Lindi Scharfstein, interior designer and project manager for Wellmont Health System, and members of the Heritage Wall Committee. The committee included Janet Brown, Deb Browning, Angela Griffith and Tony Politz. The museum is located near the main lobby of the hospital.

JULY 13, 1964

Youth Slain on Long Island

The *Kingsport News* reported that the seventeen-year-old son of an ex-convict was fatally stabbed in the chest in a fight with the seventeen-year-old son of a Long Island minister. Sam Riner was pronounced dead on arrival at Holston Valley Community Hospital, and Jerry Clark admitted to the stabbing. Clark is being held without bond on a charge of murder. Clark is the son of Long Island Primitive Baptist Church minister Garland Clark. Riner's grandfather and legal guardian, Willie Evans, said Riner had returned home for a visit from a job in Illinois working with his father, who had been released from prison a short time earlier. Witnesses said the fight started after Riner claimed Clark pushed his younger brother into the Holston River. According to Clark, the knife belonged to Riner. Riner had pulled it but dropped it on the ground. Clark picked it up and lunged at him, resulting in the stabbing.

JULY 14, 1940

WKPT On Air

The Nation's Model Station, WKPT, went on air at 5:30 p.m. on this day. Speeches by Mayor E.W. Tipton, J. Fred Johnson and Harold Gray were the highlight of the opening ceremonies. WKPT would maintain a full-time staff of twelve announcers and air seventeen hours each day. The station was managed by Harold Gray, a pioneer in radio. Gray is known from coast

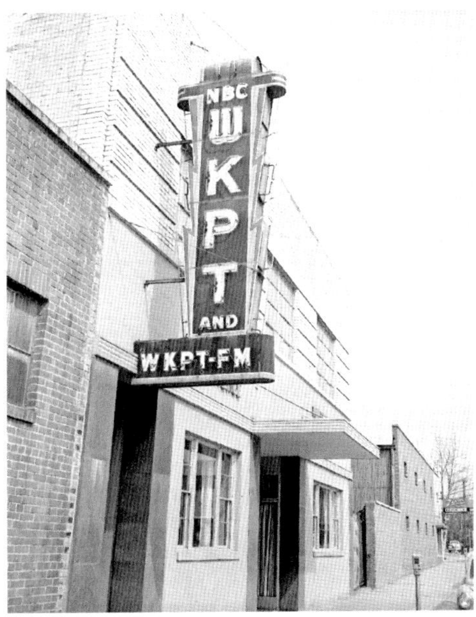

WKPT Building, Commerce Street.
Archives of the City of Kingsport.

to coast for his work as announcer in the Washington, D.C. studios of CBS. The commercial manager of the station was Harman Mosley and chief engineer was J. Guy Beard. Among the leading vocalists for the station was Dotty Breese, a graduate of Dobyns-Bennett High School already known around town for being in several dance bands. WKPT had plans for a quiz show, dramatic readings and a "Southern Hayride" series featuring hillbilly bands, acts, quartets and instrumentalists from all over.

July 15, 1930

Happy Jack

Happy Jack Eckert, the largest man in the world, appeared at a summer festival in Highland Park. Happy Jack claimed to be the biggest Elk, Moose and Woodman in the world. At 739 pounds, he held the record for the largest belly by circumference. He often appeared on stage decked out in his ceremonial garb. Happy Jack was here with a traveling side show operating the summer festival. He was among the longest living circus "fat mans" in history and died in an automobile accident in Mobile, Alabama, at sixty-three years old. The traveling show he was with in Kingsport advertised a number of rides and other attractions for "clean, wholesome entertainment."

July 16, 1923

Camp Hammond

Camp Hammond, the American Legion camp for Boy Scouts, opened for business. The camp was located about three-fourths of a mile beyond Pactolus at the juncture of Kendrick's Creek with the Holston River. A large kitchen and mess hall had been erected on the site. Three large tents had been pitched and a swimming hole prepared. The camp would consist of two periods of ten days each. The first period was for Boy Scouts, while the second period was open to all boys. Plans were being made for use of the camp by girls at some point that summer. At the end of summer, the camp would be turned over to the local high school for ten days of athletic training prior to the opening day of school. Except during rainy weather, the camp was accessible by automobile.

July 17, 1939

Singing Cowboy

Gene Autry, the singing cowboy, appeared in person at the Strand Theatre. He was supported by the comedian Frankie Marvin and the Golden West Cowboys from WSM's Grand Ole Opry. Autry was scheduled to perform five programs during the day to accommodate the crowds. Autry began his professional career as a singer when he joined a traveling medicine show at the age of fourteen. Autry had two superstitions: he refused to sing without his ten-gallon hat and completed each number with the phrase "That's it."

July 18, 1964

Crime Spree

Rufus T. Franklin and Orville Smith were arrested following a high-speed chase with police in a stolen car and a crime spree involving burglaries, thefts, vandalism and arson cases. The stolen car, a 1964 Thunderbird, was taken from Dall and Bob Motor Sales on Wilcox Drive. Other items taken from the car lot include a typewriter, an adding machine, a check writer, a clock, a radio, a heater, cookies and crackers. Police, unaware the burglary and car theft had taken place, stopped the car around 3:00 a.m. The car stopped but then sped away. Officers chased the car at speeds of one hundred miles an hour. The car overheated, and the boys abandoned it and ran into nearby woods. Shortly after coming out of the woods, they were arrested. Under questioning, Franklin admitted to a long series of thefts and other crimes. He told police that the thefts and vandalism gave him the kicks.

July 19, 2005

Ed Cifers

Edward "Ed" Clifton Cifers died on this day in Knoxville, Tennessee. Cifers, Dobyns-Bennett High School class of 1934, had an outstanding athletic career that started in high school. Cifers was the first All-State high school football selection from northeastern Tennessee. After high school, Cifers played for the University of Tennessee, where he was part of three SEC Championship teams under the direction of legendary coach Robert Neyland. Upon graduation from UT, Cifers played five seasons in the NFL with the Washington Redskins and the Chicago Bears. In 1965, he was named to *Sports Illustrated*'s Silver Anniversary All-America team and inducted to the Tennessee Sports Hall of Fame in 1983.

July 20, 1954

Medical Arts Building

The *Kingsport Times* announced the opening of the Medical Arts Pharmacy, located in the Medical Arts Building at 126 West Ravine Street. Run by Dr. C. Harry Adams, the pharmacy featured all new equipment for compounding medicines to "your doctor's exact instructions." Adams, formerly associated with Freel's Drug Store, received his pharmacy degree from the Medical College of Virginia in 1927. The pharmacy ensured that customers would receive prompt, courteous, expert service and fresh, potent products at fair prices.

July 21, 1959

Sunday Closing

Mayor L.P. Gregory announced that he had communications from five or six service station operators asking for passage of a Sunday Closing Law. Twenty-seven service station operators signed the original petition. The additions would bring the total up to thirty-two or thirty-three of the forty operating within the city limits. They asked the council to pass an ordinance requiring all service stations in the city close from midnight Saturday to midnight Sunday. This move would require motorists to use service stations in the fringe areas outside the city if they wanted to get gasoline or get a tire repaired on a Sunday. Kingsport already had a blue law in effect that restricted some business operations on Sundays. This was the first time that a request had been made to tighten the law. At this point, no formal opposition had been made.

July 22, 1949

Operation Tomcat

The *Kingsport Times* reported on this day about Operation Tomcat, a rather interesting saga between a bird nicknamed Marauder and a cat named Sawdust. According to Mr. John D. Barker, operator of a cabinet shop, about a week ago, the bird started launching aerial attacks on Sawdust the moment he was on all fours. The bird wouldn't attack if Sawdust was lying under a tree, only when his paws were on the ground. No one was sure what species the bird was. At first, it was thought to be an adult mockingbird, but after the report on Operation Tomcat came out, it was noted that it more than likely was a shrike, or butcher bird. Shortly after the story was published in the paper, the *Kingsport Times* began receiving similar reports of birds attacking throughout Kingsport.

July 23, 1925

McPheter's Bend Movie Show

A large crowd was in attendance this evening for a free moving picture show at McPheter's Bend sponsored by the Dobyns-Taylor Hardware Company. The crowd began to assemble around 7:00 p.m., and by the time the movie started around 8:00 p.m., there were nearly five hundred people in attendance. The show was a rare treat seldom afforded in the country. The movie, which pertained to farm life and provided new and helpful hints, was a novelty to many of the attending farmers and their families.

July 24, 1925

Mrs. Geiger Jumps off the Rotherwood Bridge

Mrs. E.M. Geiger ended her life on this day by throwing herself off the Rotherwood Bridge into the Holston River. It is believed that Mrs. Geiger had become despondent over her ill health. Geiger apparently called a taxi to take her to Rotherwood from her home on Ravine Street. On the way to Rotherwood, she asked taxi driver Bailey Light to stop at the home of Mrs. Bellamy. At the Bellamy home, Geiger left a diamond ring with Mrs. Bellamy and then continued to Rotherwood. Finding the exchange rather odd, Mrs. Bellamy informed Mrs. F.L. Cloud, who then informed her husband, city manager Frank Cloud. Cloud and T.R. Bandy tracked down the taxi driver to learn where Geiger had been dropped off. They then went to Rotherwood, where they discovered her body. Mrs. Geiger was survived by her husband, E.M. Geiger, local manager of the Standard Oil Company, and her mother, Mrs. Mollie Whitlock.

July 25, 1954

Ridgefields Golfing Exhibition

One of the largest crowds for a golfing exhibition was expected today according to Bill Jordan, chairman of the Ridgefields Country Club Tournament Committee. Golf pros Billy Joe Platton and Gene Littler were at the golf course to play in a foursome with Jack Shelley and Joe Cheves. Shelley was the Ridgefields pro, and Cheves was Patton's home pro at Morgantown, North Carolina. The match was open to the public, not just members of Ridgefields. The Ridgefields Country Club opened its golf course with nine holes in June 1949, and the rest of the course was opened in 1950. The Ridgefields Golf Course was planned by golf course designer Donald Ross. Ross was involved in designing and redesigning over four hundred golf courses in the course of his career.

July 26, 2005

Blazier-Wilson Hall

Dr. John Locke hosted the building dedication of the new Blazier-Wilson Hall in downtown Kingsport. The building opened as one of the first buildings of the Kingsport Academic Village. The Kingsport Academic Village is a center for higher education and workforce development in downtown Kingsport. Blazier-Wilson Hall, on West Main Street, is named after Keith Wilson of the *Kingsport Times-News* and former mayor Jeanette Blazier. The two conceived the idea and spent several years trying to appropriate the funds and raise money.

July 27, 1925

Kingsport Foundry and Machine Works

Kingsport Foundry and Machine Works was officially opened for business on this day. The modern foundry and machine shop was located on the property of the old dye plant. At a recent stockholder meeting, the officers and directors were elected. H.C. Massengill was elected president; James Berger, vice-president; and B.C. Pendleton, secretary-treasurer. The directors were J.A. Cross, R. Fisher, W.T. Jones (general manager), W.R. Jennings, James Berger and H.C. Massengill. The foundry and machine shop were equipped with the latest equipment and skilled mechanics.

July 28, 1933

Mrs. J. Fred Johnson Dies

Ruth Carter Johnson, wife of J. Fred Johnson, passed away this morning at her home on Watauga Street. Mrs. Johnson's death came after an illness of about nine months. Mrs. Johnson, the daughter of Walter and Lucy Carter of Hillsville, Virginia, married J. Fred Johnson in 1896. She was the sister of George L. Carter, a rail and coal magnate and founder of modern

Kingsport. Mrs. Johnson was a prominent figure in early Kingsport, involved in a number of organizations and clubs that helped shape Kingsport. Mrs. Johnson was a member of the First Presbyterian Church, where she had taught a women's Bible class consistently since the organization of the church. Besides her husband and brother, Mrs. Johnson was survived by two sisters, Mrs. M.W. Doggett, wife of Reverend M.W. Doggett of Kingsport, and Mrs. R.G. Wilkinson of Hillsville.

July 29, 1940

Landmark Gets Facelift

The Broad Street Methodist Church's bell tower, one of the city's oldest landmarks, underwent a good cleaning and repair by workmen on this day. The cleaning was done mostly in preparation of new coping and gutters. Designed at the same time Kingsport was laid out, Broad Street Methodist is among the city's oldest churches. J.W. Dobyns, first mayor of Kingsport, shoveled the first spadesful of dirt during the excavation for the church. During World War I, Kingsporters of all denominations gathered at the church daily to pray for peace.

July 30, 1929

McCracken Sentenced to Reformatory

Eugene McCracken, fourteen, was sentenced this morning to serve six years in the State Reformatory in Nashville, Tennessee. Juvenile judge Collins handed down the sentence stemming from charges of breaking into the Mouiten and Minnich Feed Store located on Market Street. McCracken was arrested by officers in Johnson City and confessed to the crime. He was brought back to Kingsport to face charges. Officer Clay Crawford with the Kingsport Police Department noted that the youth had been giving police a lot of trouble. McCracken would later be tried for the murder of Kingsport policeman J.E. Mills. McCracken's life of crime began at the age of eleven, when he was convicted of stealing an automobile.

July 31, 1933

Raises for Employees

Starting on this day, Dobyns-Taylor Hardware Company employees would receive an average twenty-five-cent wage increase, as the organization put to effect the presidential reemployment agreement. Dobyns-Taylor was the first Kingsport organization to sign the blanket code and send to Washington. The presidential reemployment agreement issued under President Franklin D. Roosevelt was part of a nationwide plan to raise wages and create employment, thus increasing purchasing power and restoring commerce. On top of the wage increase, Dobyns-Taylor would be adding four new employees, making the total of employees around twenty-eight. The agreement affected workers in the hardware, mill supply, household equipment, furniture and gift departments. Dobyns-Taylor planned to maintain its regular hours of operation.

AUGUST

August 1, 1950

Kingsport Jailbreak

Two prisoners managed to break out of the Kingsport City Jail by sawing their way through three iron bars in the rear cellblock of the jail. The two men, Paul White and Robert Harkelroad, made their break between 7:00 and 9:00 p.m. Cecil Ammons, desk officer, reported that Harkelroad had visitors around 7:15 p.m. There were about ten other men in the cell at the time of the escape, but they chose to stay behind. They were moved to a different cell when the escape was noticed. Officers received a call around 9:30 p.m. that two men had jumped from an automobile with North Carolina license plates and caught a freight train. Harkelroad had been in jail on charges of reckless driving, driving without a license and an old fine. White was in for charges on an old fine of fifteen dollars.

August 2, 1948

Special Meeting Called

A special meeting for all members of the Charles DeWitt Byrd Post No. 3382 of the Veterans of Foreign Wars was called on this day. The meeting, held at 8:00 p.m. at the post house, was called to discuss matters, including the possibility of the VFW participating in the upcoming county general election and party primaries. The VFW post was named for Charles DeWitt Byrd, the first from Kingsport to die in World War II. Byrd joined the navy in October 1940 and was stationed at Pearl Harbor on the day it was attacked. The Kingsport native and Dobyns-Bennett High School graduate was aboard the USS *Arizona*.

August 3, 1916

No Better Water

The *Kingsport Times* announced on this day that waterworks and a sewage system would be started soon. The water would come from Bays Mountain: "Large clear, cold springs will be turned into a reservoir and pipes will bring the mountain water fresh from the fountain to Kingsport. No better water in East Tennessee." J. Fred Johnson, one of Kingsport's early leaders, began buying land on Bays Mountain to eventually create a lake to be used as Kingsport's water source. By 1914, Johnson had sold the land to the Kingsport Waterworks Corporation, which promptly began work on the dam. Bays Mountain's lake served as the source of Kingsport's water until 1944, when the city outgrew the lake's capacity.

August 4, 1953

BMA Approves Mother Patrol

The Kingsport School Mother Patrol was approved by the BMA. The patrol, begun with three women on a trial basis, worked to control and direct traffic in and around school zones. The women worked about fifteen hours a week and were paid sixty dollars a month. According to the August 5, 1953 edition of the *Kingsport Times-News*, "[T]hey would be regular traffic officers in every sense except they will work on a part-time basis. They will have the same authority as other police to make arrests and issue court summonses for traffic violations and will prosecute their cases in city court the same as the full-time policeman." The Mother Patrol paved the way for Kingsport's first full-time patrolwoman, Mrs. Harriett Grills. Grills was on the Mother Patrol squad, then hired in 1954 to work full time on parking violations.

August 5, 1950

State Theater Ticket Booth Robbed

The State Theater ticket booth, with Hazel Cox working, was robbed around 6:45 p.m. The State Theater was located on Broad Street. The robber was Dallan Fritz, twenty, of Old Kingsport. Hazel Cox, with a .28 pistol pointed at her, gave Fritz the money. Shoving the money in his pocket, Fritz fled south down Broad Street and turned right at the alley between Dobyns-Taylor Hardware Company and Kingsport Fruit and News. Patrolman Everett Dykes, who happened to be nearby, heard someone shout, "There goes the man who robbed the State Theater." Dykes took chase and captured Fritz on Shelby Street. Fritz was taken to Holston Valley Community Hospital, where he was treated for a gunshot wound. Dykes, although chasing Fritz with a gun drawn, never fired. Fritz stumbled and accidently shot himself in the leg.

August 6, 1954

Coke Party

Martha Goerdel, bride-elect of Gayle Dunning, was honored at a coke party this morning at the Ridgefields Country Club. Mrs. Haywood, aunt of Mr. Dunning, was the hostess. The refreshment table was overlaid with white linen and centered with a bouquet of red zinnias. Miss Goerdel wore a green linen dress topped with a white linen jacket and a corsage of pink rosebuds. Guests at the event included Mrs. Karl Goerdel, Mrs. Dunning, Mrs. Clifton Hamlett, Mrs. L.J. Felton, Mrs. Kyle Huddle, Mrs. D.C. Lionberger, Mrs. Donald Fauble, Mrs. Leslie R. Etchison, Mrs. James W. Gunn, Mrs. Robert Bingham, Miss Joann Emmert, Miss June Emmert, Miss Phyllis Brockman, Miss Kay Modlin and Miss Lois Dryden.

AUGUST 7, 1946

Soapbox Derby

The first soapbox derby in Kingsport occurred on this day. The race took place on Oak Street Hill with sixty-three entrants. Sponsored by the Latimer-Looney Chevrolet Company and the *Kingsport Times-News*, the derby was open to all boys ages eleven to fifteen. The Monday prior to the race was the final and official inspection of the vehicles by J.S. Turpin of Latimer-Looney, chief inspector. All derby cars were inspected for weight, size and cost and to see if official derby rules were followed. After inspection, the cars were locked in the recreation room at the Civic Auditorium. This was to ensure no cars were tampered with after they passed inspection. There was a crowd of around three thousand for the race. Dickie Blankenbeckler and Ed Hyder were the first racers in inaugural event, and Gary McGinnis was declared the first soapbox derby winner. Richard "Dickie" Warren came in a close second.

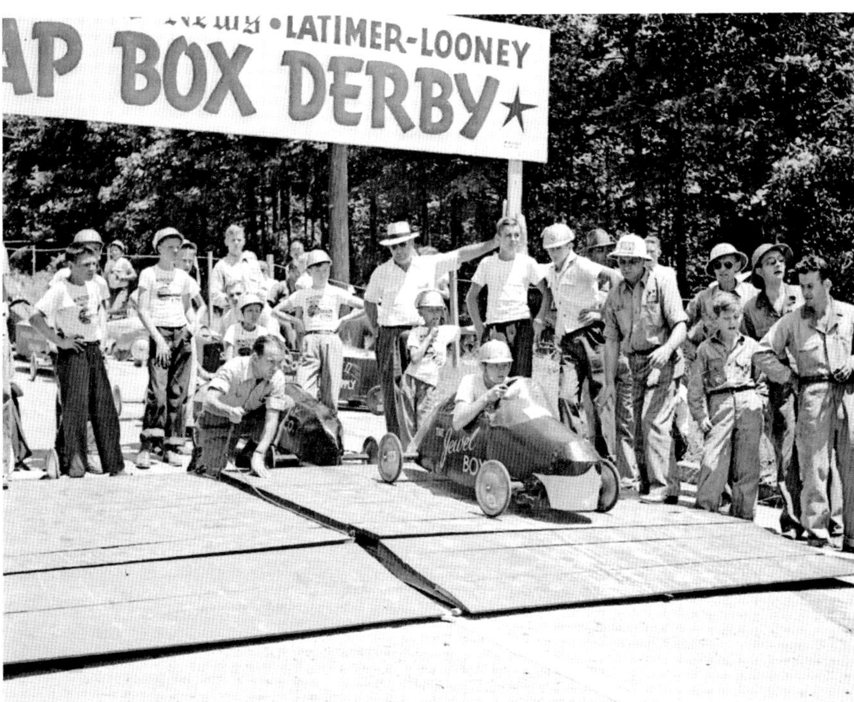

Soapbox derby. *Archives of the City of Kingsport.*

August 8, 1981

Fun Fest

The very first Fun Fest opened on this day in 1981 to the theme of "Community Unity." The concert for this first year featured Margie and Marcie Cates and Ray Stevens. "Fun Fest was created as an effort to unite Kingsport residents, to help foster a belief that Kingsport is a caring community that is a good place to live and to work, and to provide numerous opportunities for people to congregate and become acquainted while appealing to their interests in culture, athletics, arts and entertainment."

August 9, 1935

Holston Valley Community Hospital Dedicated

The dedication of Holston Valley Community Hospital occurred on this day. The hospital had fifty-three beds and nine bassinets when it was opened. The vision of the hospital actually began to take shape decades before it was built. Early city leaders and planners picked the site of the hospital and never wavered in the belief that a hospital would be built there one day. Once construction started, the facility took about fifteen months to complete. The building was equipped with the latest in medical equipment and considered one of the greatest institutions in the South.

August 10, 1931

Swank and Smith Charged

Acting on a warrant sworn out before magistrate J.H. Jones of Greenback, Tennessee, Constable McTeer of Blount County arrived in Kingsport on this day to arrest E.A. Swank and E.H. Smith. Swank and Smith were charged with obtaining money under false pretense. The former employees of the Industrial Savings and Loan Bank of Morristown obtained $5,000 in U.S. Liberty Bonds from a Mrs. Griffith under the implication that they were still employed by the bank. Swank was one of the organizers of a newly proposed industrial bank to be located in the Farmers and Merchants Bank building in Downtown Kingsport.

August 11, 1932

Kingsport Utilities Building Dedicated

The dedication of the new Kingsport Utilities building on Church Circle was scheduled for 3:00 p.m. on this day. The ceremony was presided over by C.A. Thornburg, general manager of the Kingsport Utilities Company, a subsidiary of the American Glass and Electric Company. Following the dedication, the newly constructed building was open for tours. It originally housed the Kingsport Power Company and was constructed to be architecturally similar to the Kingsport Public Library building located next door. The building underwent a renovation several years ago to become the home of Tri-Summit Bank.

August 12, 1950

Daylight Holdup

Two men were arraigned in general sessions court on charges of armed robbery. Judge Sidney Gilbreath set their bonds at $50,000 each. The arraignment came after James F. Ashbury and Guy H. Culbertson, officials of Dobyns-Taylor Hardware Company, identified the pair as two of the three men who held them up in front of the Strand Theatre and robbed them of $25,741.94, which they were carrying from the First National Bank to the store. The men, Harry Daniels, aka John McGhee or James Collins, and Benjamin Ristine Jr., were arrested in Knoxville and brought to Kingsport. The robbery occurred in broad daylight, and the getaway car was parked in a no-parking zone in front of the theater. Police were confident that the crime had been solved.

AUGUST 13, 1950

Bootleggers Leaving the Area

Reports from sources close to liquor traffickers in the Kingsport area said dealers in bootleg whiskey were currently making plans to move their places of business out of Sullivan County and into Hawkins County or Virginia. The moves were planned to occur before September 1, which is when Ham Hurd, newly elected Sullivan County sheriff, would be sworn in. During his campaign, Hurd promised to clean up Sullivan County, and the underworld apparently took him at his word. Prior to the election, Hurd was approached with several offers to make deals with some of the dealers in illicit liquor, but he warned them to "get"—or else.

AUGUST 14, 1940

Long Island Flood

Kingsport experienced its worst flood in over thirty-nine years; damage was estimated to be well over $50,000. The Long Island and Stabtown sections of town were hit the hardest and suffered the most damage. The warning

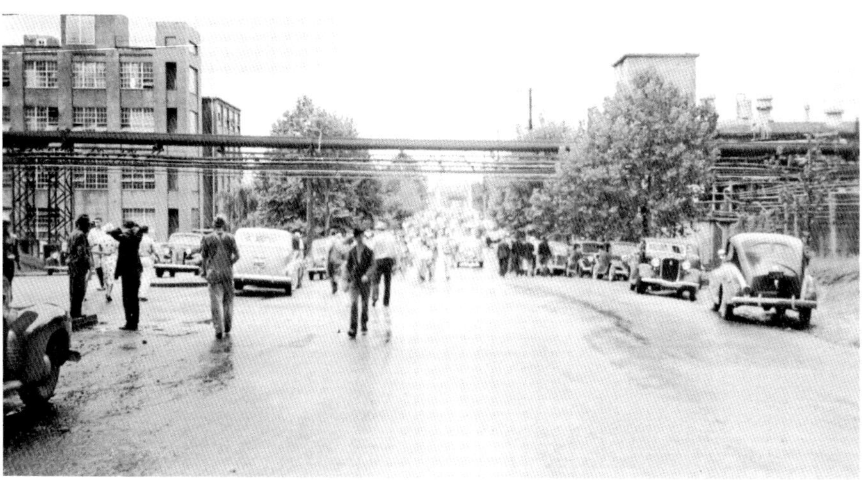

Scene from the flood on Long Island. *Archives of the City of Kingsport.*

alarm that sounded hours before the Holston River began to rise was credited with significantly preventing loss of life. The alarm was sounded around 1:30 a.m., and city and county officers, Red Cross workers, Boy Scouts, local volunteers and state highway patrolmen began assisting residents of Long Island and Old Kingsport in evacuating the area. Local taxi companies aided the removal of residents by furnishing free fares. Around 114 people took refuge at the Civic Auditorium, and many local restaurants provided free food for refugees of the flood. At its highest peak, the floodwaters measured fourteen and one quarter feet at the Eastman Bridge.

August 15, 1931

The Great Nemar

A crowd of twenty-five thousand was reported to have been on hand to witness the amazing, blindfolded drive of the "Great Nemar" through the streets of Kingsport. Nemar, acclaimed the world's greatest blind driver, drove a Plymouth sedan from the Mills Motor Company for his stunt. Nemar was blindfolded with silver dollars strapped with tape over his eyes. Over the tape was placed a copper mask held in place by a heavy black cloth. According to Nemar, the feat was performed through telepathic contact with Madame Nemar, who rode in a car immediately following the one he was driving. George Hillard of Kingsport Sheet Metal Works made the mask that Nemar used in his blindfolded drive.

August 16, 1926

Fair Acres

Announcements were made today concerning the development of the 250-acre tract of land in the Dobyns Addition. The development was set to become a beautiful residential section called Fair Acres on land owned and controlled by S.F. Dobyns, B.E. Dobyns and their mother, Mrs. J.W. Dobyns. The work had been in development for the last few months, but the announcement only became public today. Besides the residences in

Fair Acres, the plan included a park and playgrounds. Circling the whole 250-acre tract would be a street known as Crescent Drive. According to S.F. Dobyns, "When completed, Fair Acres will be an exclusive high-class residential section unsurpassed in beauty."

August 17, 1966

Father of Thirteen Jailed

A Kingsport man, Robert Condry, was jailed today for failure to support his wife and thirteen children after he was arrested in a raid on a home in Long Island. Condry had failed to pay the thirty dollars a week the court had ordered him to pay his wife, Nadine. Nadine had sworn out a warrant against Condry on charges of abandonment. The couple had thirteen children, only four of which lived at home. The following year, Robert Condry was shot to death at the home of Marie Fields on Long Island. Fields was charged with murder, but the grand jury did not indict her because of her claims that Condry had approached her with a knife and she shot him in self-defense. This was the second time Condry had been shot by Fields. The first time was in 1965, when she shot him in the foot. Condry decided to not press charges in that incident.

August 18, 1931

Community Chest

At a meeting this morning by officials of the Kingsport Community Chest, it was announced that approximately $9,000 had been raised in two days' work. That amount is half of the $18,000 quota the Community Chest had hoped to raise. Chest executives were confident the rest of the amount could be raised by the upcoming Saturday. The Community Chest began in 1922 as a Kingsport Men's Business Club fundraiser, and it was chartered in 1934. In 1988, the Community Chest became the United Way of Greater Kingsport.

August 19, 1927

Harman and Bain Dance

Two prominent citizens of Kingsport, Walter Harman and John Bain, treated locals with an exhibition of dancing on Broad Street. Music was furnished by a blind fiddler. The enthusiastic crowd cheered Harmon and Bain on. Many in the audience suggested that Harman and Bain start a dancing team and immediately start booking for road performances.

August 20, 1938

Lawn Party

Mabel Moore and Zoe Turner were joint hostesses at a lawn party given at the home of Mrs. T.R. Turner. Games were played and contests held; Ruby Good and Joe Good won prizes. The following guests attended the party: Sallie Taylor, Myrtle Lee Taylor, Vera Sue Kilgore, Vivian Rasnick, Lucille Dotson, Anna Bell Porter, Nannie Maude Horner, Fae Burke, Kathaline Burke, Sarah Addington, Evelyn Meade, Fannie Kilgore, Reta Minton, Ruby Good, Maxie White, Neva Campbell, Dorothy Moore, Ubert McConnell, Junior Whited, Carl McConnell, Joe Good, Howard Moore, Roy Buchannan, Ed Minton, Luther Dean, Ellis Taylor, Lester Kiser, Henry Kilgore, Sylvester Dean, Whales Harris, Harmon Ed Davenport, Herbert Fielder, Alfred Stapleton, Joe Moore, Otis Blankenbelcher, Bob Taylor and Frank Bays. The music for the party was furnished by Howard Moore, Carl McConnell and Joe Good. Late-hour dainty refreshments were served.

August 21, 1822

Charter of 1822

Kingsport was originally chartered on this day. At the time, Kingsport was an important shipping port on the Holston River. Goods originating for many miles from the surrounding countryside were loaded onto barges for the journey downriver to the Tennessee River at Knoxville. This era of Kingsport's history is more commonly referred to as "Old Kingsport," since the modern charter was signed in 1917. Kingsport lost its original charter shortly after the Civil War, when the area suffered greatly.

August 22, 1935

First Operation

Kathleen Hutchins Moseley, twenty-one, of Bristol Highway, was the first person to undergo an operation at the new Holston Valley Community Hospital. Moseley, wife of Ralph Moseley and daughter of Dr. and Mrs. Hutchins, had an appendix operation performed by Drs. W.H. Reed and M.J. Adams. The hospital reported her condition as "good." In addition to being the first to be operated on, Moseley was the first to use the new combination ether and gas device installed in the new hospital.

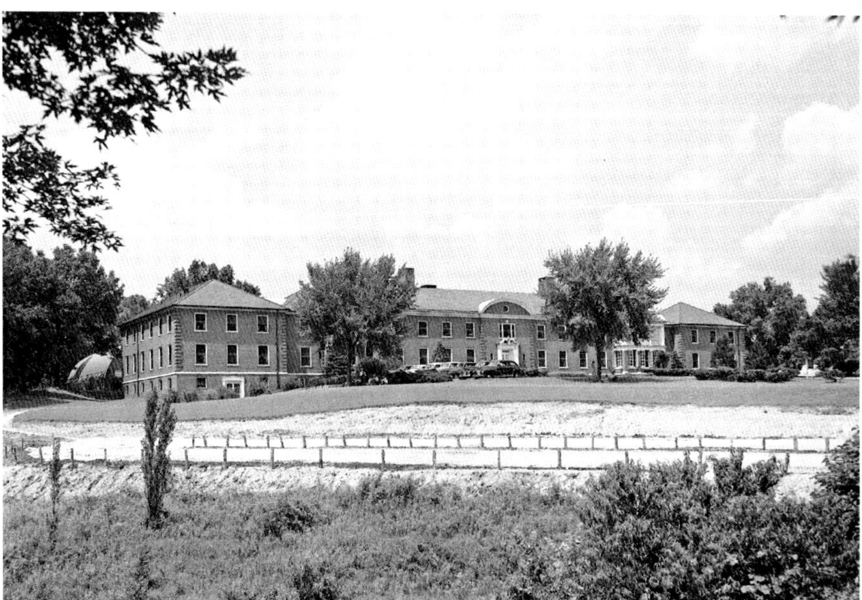

Holston Valley Community Hospital. *Archives of the City of Kingsport.*

August 23, 1994

MeadowView

The MeadowView Conference and Convention Center celebrated its original groundbreaking on this day. To celebrate the event, a "shooting of the anvil" was reenacted for attendees that included dozens of statewide and local dignitaries. The groundbreaking began at 11:00 a.m., with an invocation given by Reverend Danny Morris and the National Anthem sung by Paul Patterson. Alderwoman Sarah Lou Ring, chairman of the groundbreaking committee, gave the introduction and welcome to attendees.

August 24, 1953

East Tennessee District Fair

Today marked the opening day of this year's East Tennessee District Fair and Horse Show. A total of about $21,000 in prize money had been set aside for various contests. Over $7,000 of the money was allocated to the horse show. This year's fair featured atomic energy exhibitions, livestock exhibitions and various contests. The tractor-driving contest was the first

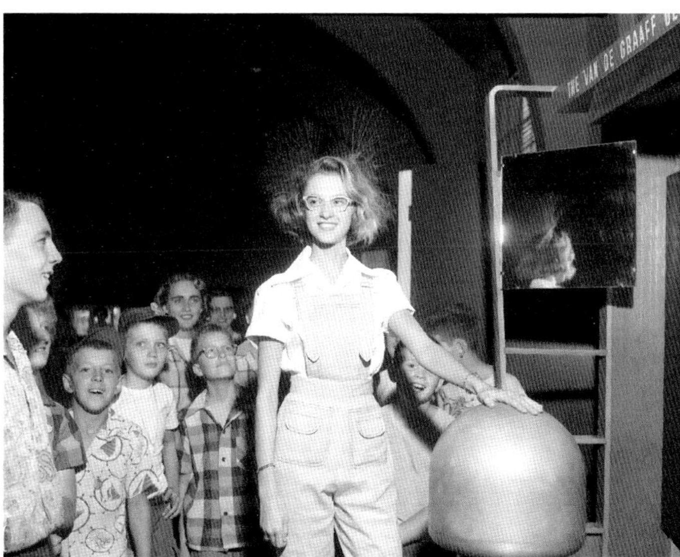

Betty Pendleton demonstrates the Van de Graaff generator during the atomic energy show at the 1953 East Tennessee District Fair. *Archives of the City of Kingsport.*

contest of the fair. Carolyn Adams was chosen as queen to reign over the fifth annual district fair. The executive committee of the East Tennessee District Fair Association consisted of Jack King (president), John Poteat (first vice-president), A.S. Brooks (second vice-president), Philip Shivell (secretary), L.P. Gregory (treasurer), J.A. Clark, Scott Roller and W.E. Wright.

August 25, 1939

Passerby Saves Falling Man

J.C. Cowden escaped possible serious injury when a passerby caught him as he toppled off scaffolding twelve feet above the ground. Cowden, an employee of the firm remodeling the Clinchfield Drug Store, was working on the scaffolding as he was placing a piece of Carrara glass on the building. Cowden lost his footing and toppled over backward. Lucky for him, H.M. McNeil was standing on the corner and noticed Cowden's predicament. McNeil rushed over and was able to catch Cowden, sparing him from injury. Several years before this incident, Jack Agee, an electrician, was working on scaffolding in front of the same building when he fell off and was fatally injured.

August 26, 1919

Rotherwood Elm Dying

The world's largest, and possibly oldest, elm tree, the Rotherwood Elm, was dying. The *Kingsport Times* reported on this day that the elm at Kingsport Farms in Rotherwood was failing. J. Fred Johnson, with an interest in preserving the tree, visited Washington, D.C., to confer with the Forestry Department but was advised to take the matter to the state level. A representative from the state came to access the tree, and Johnson requested a tree surgeon to be sent to try to save the tree. The Rotherwood Elm was reported to have been first mentioned as early as 1790 by historians as being one of the most wonderful trees in the country. The trunk of the tree measured 22 feet in circumference, and the branches had a spread of over 150 feet.

August 27, 1929

Fred Gladson Succumbs to Typhoid Fever

Fred Gladson, fifteen, the only son of Hugh W. and Lee Charles Gladson, died of typhoid fever at the home of his parents in Sevier Terrace. Gladson was a popular student at Dobyns-Bennett High School, and his funeral was conducted the following day at the Broad Street Methodist Church. A large crowd attended the service, and a large and beautiful floral offering was placed on his casket. Active pallbearers were W.K. Nelms, Elbert Hurt, Frank Umberger, Dowe Fitzgerald, John Barnes and James Dean. Hugh Gladson was the owner and operator of Gladson Service Station on the corner of East Center and Oak Streets.

August 28, 1973

Richard Watterson

On this day, Richard Watterson became the first African American to be elected to the board of mayor and aldermen. Watterson graduated from Douglass High School and served in the U.S. Navy from 1943 to 1946; he spent most of his time on the USS *Nassau*. After attending Swift Memorial Junior College, Watterson served many community organizations, including the State Board of Legal Services, State Commissioner for Human Development and the board of directors of the Kingsport Boy's Club; he was also the first chairman of the Riverview Branch Boy's Club. Watterson served as an alderman from 1973 to 1997 and as vice-mayor from 1981 to 1995. During his service on the BMA, Richard was a tireless leader for growth and modernization.

August 29, 1919

Centenary Revival

Kingsport's two Methodist churches came together for a day of fasting and prayer for a church-wide centenary revival. The entire membership of both churches was expected to fast and pray. One objective of the Methodist Centenary Movement was the revival of the spiritual life of its members and constituents. Churches all over the country participated in this nationwide event. Locally, the Holston Conference wanted to double its membership in five years. The membership in the Holston Conference in 1919 was more than eighty thousand.

August 30, 1927

Harve Hensley Jailed

Local deputy sheriffs Paul L. and T.L. Thompson, along with Officer Bailey of Knoxville, arrested Harve Hensley on charges of abduction and concubinage. Hensley was discovered at his father's home on Island Home in Knoxville. The warrant against Hensley charged him with leaving Kingsport with his fourteen-year-old sister-in-law while his wife was confined to her home in West View Park. The girl taken by Hensley was found at the home in Knoxville but ill from typhoid fever. Hensley was returned to Kingsport.

August 31, 1989

Blake Leeper

Patrick "Blake" Leeper, a U.S. Paralympic athlete, was born on this day. Leeper was born with both legs missing below the knee and has worn prosthetics since nine months of age. In his childhood, Blake participated in various sports—baseball, basketball and others—with his dad coaching. Leeper, a Dobyns-Bennett High School graduate, was a member of the high school basketball team. Leeper is an eight-time Paralympic track and field international medalist, world record holder and three-time American record holder. He was chosen to represent the United States in the 2016 Paralympics in Rio de Janeiro, Brazil.

SEPTEMBER

September 1, 1917

Car Thieves

Automobile thieves took a car belonging to Dr. Givens out to Rotherwood and removed all four tires, two wheels and the radiator. Dr. Givens had reported the car stolen from where it had been parked in front of his home. The car was found under the traffic bridge at Rotherwood, and the police reportedly had no clues as to the identity of the thieves.

September 2, 1932

Money Mad

Money Mad, a comedy show, was presented at the Dobyns-Bennett High School Auditorium. The program was sponsored by the Parent Teacher Association and featured a variety of acts and performers for the show they called "a screamingly funny comedy." The comedy was clean cut and filled with laughs and promised to be one of the cleverest shows ever staged at the high school. The story revolved around a rich uncle played by Tom Warrick who promises his nephew $50,000 providing he stays single until he is thirty-five. The nephew, played by Bill Gilmer, ends up falling for a girl, played by Margaret Nelms. The minstrel part of the show included members of the Kingsport Men's Business Club.

September 3, 1947

Bobby Blake at the State

Robert "Bobby" Blake was in Kingsport today and appeared in a stage show at the State Theater. Blake, the twelve-year-old actor who plays the part of Little Beaver in the Red Ryder movies was made an honorary member of the State Theater Popeye Club. Farley Green, theater manager, presented him with his membership certificate in front of a crowd of fans waiting for autographs and photographs. Blake appeared as a child actor in twenty-two entries of the Red Ryder film franchise. As an adult, he became well known for his appearance as Tony Baretta in the TV show *Baretta*. In 2005, Blake was tried and acquitted for the murder of his second wife, Bonnie Lee Bakley.

September 4, 1965

Cotillion

The Voguette's Social Sewing Club presented the First Annual Debutante Cotillion Spectacular at the Civic Auditorium. The debutantes included Patricia Bristol, Charlotte Young, Joy Hankins, Huphelia Lollar, Gayle Turner, Jewel Davis, Melrose Dobbins, Andrea Watterson, Linda Miller, Phyllis Horton, Pamela Rutledge, Sharon Lindsay, Darlene Marble, Rowena Foster, Geneva Ross and Carolyn Dulaney. The Voguette's Social Sewing Club began in 1951 at the home of Mrs. Inez Ervin. The official motto of the club was "Every woman can become greater than she is."

SEPTEMBER 5, 1957

Test of Eastman Superglue

An impressive test of Eastman Superglue was held on this day. Peter Morison and Paul Van Bramer, employees of Eastman, used one drop of the adhesive between two cylinders. After a thirty-minute cure time, the steel-steel bond supported a weight of over two and a half tons. This was demonstrated by lifting a car with three passengers inside. Superglue, also known as Eastman No. 910, was invented by Eastman employee Dr. Harry W. Coover Jr. and put on the market in 1958. In 2010, Coover was awarded National Medal of Technology and Innovation by President Obama for inventing Superglue. Coover held around 460 patents in his lifetime and was inducted into the National Inventors Hall of Fame in 2004. Dr. Coover died in 2011.

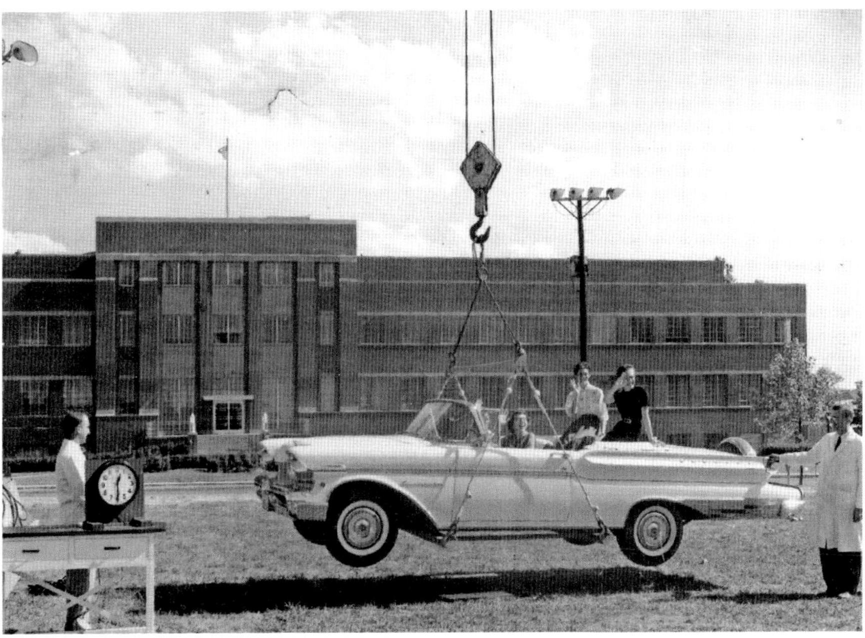

Peter Morison and Paul Van Bramer test Eastman Superglue in front of Tennessee Eastman Research Building. *Archives of the City of Kingsport.*

September 6, 1930

Baseball Banquet

The Borden Mill Recreation Association Baseball Banquet was held on this night at the Kingsport Inn. The banquet honored the Borden Mill, Mead and Tennessee Eastman baseball teams. The menu for the evening featured Florida fruit cocktail, cream of tomato soup, hearts of celery, sweet mixed pickles, small sirloin steak with mushroom sauce, English brown potatoes, corn fritters, tomatoes stuffed with coleslaw, hot rolls, chocolate parfait, coffee, cigars and cigarettes. Dr. D.W. Daniels, director of the arts and science department, Clemson College, provided the entertainment for the evening. The Reverend J.L. Trent gave the invocation.

September 7, 1940

Kingsport Cop killed

John Elisha Mills, a thirty-year-old member of the Kingsport Police Department, was shot during an ambush and instantly killed. The shooting prompted the launching of the greatest manhunt in Sullivan County. Police officers were called in from surrounding counties in search of two brothers, Eugene and Wayland McCracken, wanted in connection of the shooting. The McCracken brothers had only recently escaped from the jail in Bristol and were spotted in the area where Mills was killed. Mills was engaged to Miss Beatrice Henley, seventeen, of Elizabeth Street. He had previously been employed by the Kingsport Fire Department but was appointed to the Kingsport Police Department in May 1938. Eugene McCracken was later convicted of the murder and sentenced to life in prison.

September 8, 1947

Midget Auto Derby

Billy Greene of Watauga Street, led four other contestants and came in first in a homemade "automobile" race on Belmeade Drive. The five contestants were all members of the Cub Pack 54, sponsored by the Kiwanis Club under the leadership of Harry Ford. Other entrants besides Greene were Al Dryden, Walton Sproles, Bill Ford and Fritz Pilgrim. The contestants were too young to enter the soapbox derby, so the midget auto derby idea was sprung. All five boys made the miniature racers themselves. Prizes were donated by the W.B. Greene Company, Free Service Tire Company, Goodrich Tire Company, the Sport Shop, Kingsport Electric Company, Huddle Electric Company and the *Kingsport Times-News*.

September 9, 1950

Selwa Showker Roosevelt

A reception was given for Selwa Showker "Lucky" Roosevelt and Archibald B. Roosevelt Jr. (grandson of Teddy Roosevelt) at the home of the bride's parents, Mr. and Mrs. Saleem L. Showker. The reception was to honor the couple, who were just married several days before. Mrs. Roosevelt wore her wedding dress, a gown of white Chantilly lace. Guests were served an ice course and punch. The couple, along with Mr. and Mrs. Showker, formed the receiving line and welcomed nearly four hundred guests throughout the reception. Following the reception, the Roosevelts returned to New York. Mrs. Roosevelt was chief of protocol of the United States for President Ronald Reagan for almost seven years, from 1982 to 1989, longer than anyone who has served in that position. In 2012, Roosevelt received a commendation from President Barack Obama for her service to her community, country and government.

September 10, 1938

John Palmer

John Spencer Palmer was born on this day. Palmer, a 1954 graduate of Dobyns-Bennett, was a longtime news correspondent for NBC News. He started his broadcasting experience as the student radio announcer of Friday night broadcasts from Dobyns-Bennett High School. Palmer was a graduate of Northwestern University and held a master's degree from Columbia University. In an interview shortly after retirement, Palmer stated, "I was enriched as a kid from the East Tennessee Mountains…to be able to go fishing with Jimmy Carter, to go to the movies with Ronald Reagan and to play golf with Bill Clinton." John Palmer died on August 3, 2013.

September 11, 1949

Emmitt Hammonds

The *Kingsport Times-News* reported that the Kingsport Police Department was baffled by the slaying case of Emmitt Hammonds, a Plymouth cab driver. Hammonds had been found dead in his cab in Riverview several days before. One suspect, identified by Miss Bess Penley of Gibsontown, was being held while officers gathered information and looked for more witnesses. Miss Penley told police she was with Hammonds on the night in question but had run away from the scene shortly before Hammonds's death. The police department also noted that an earlier plan to administer truth serum to Miss Penley was abandoned after they decided that she would not consent to the procedure. The case remained dormant for about thirteen months, until Miss Penley herself was arrested for the murder. She was found guilty of voluntary manslaughter and sentenced to two years in the state penitentiary. Her case was under appeal by the state supreme court.

September 12, 1951

Dedication Ceremonies of Saint Dominic's School

Construction of the Saint Dominic's School building in 1950 was hampered by several setbacks. The greatest of all was that there were no available bricks following the war. The sisters and students recited the rosary together daily, commending the work on the new school to the foundress of the Sisters of Mercy, Mother Catherine McAuley. To make the plea complete, a medal of her likeness was dropped into a trowel full of cement for the cinderblock. Shortly following these acts of prayer, the pastor, Father Woodley, received word that miraculously the Johnson City Brick Yard would be sending a carload of bricks every other week. The school building was dedicated on this day.

September 13, 1934

Kingsport Book Club

The Kingsport Book Club held its first meeting after the summer vacation at the home of Mrs. E.W. Tipton on Watauga Street. There were seventeen members and one visitor present. The president of the book club, Mrs. J.C. White, gave the roll, which was answered by each member briefly reviewing the book, short story or article that she had most enjoyed during the club's vacation. Mrs. Felix Guenther gave a talk on "The Origin and Science of Heraldry" that was followed by a display of family coats of arms by the members. A social hour concluded the meeting. The Kingsport Book Club organized in 1919 under the leadership of five women: Mrs. H.J. Shivell, Mrs. S.P. Platt, Mrs. George MacNaughton, Mrs. L.A. DaShiell and Mrs. Karl Koeniger.

September 14, 1940

Borden Mill Employee Killed

Andrew Jackson Roberts, a twenty-three-year-old Borden Mill worker, died as the result of a brain hemorrhage caused by a blow to the head by John

Moseley. According to reports, Roberts arrived at the factory to start his third shift at 10:00 p.m., and Mosley, a guard at the factory, refused entry to Roberts. Some kind of altercation followed. Roberts was struck in the head with an empty soft drink bottle and taken home but was later rushed to the hospital when his parents could not wake him. He died as surgeons were preparing to operate to relieve pressure on his brain. Moseley was arrested on first-degree murder charges.

September 15, 1927

Merry Garden Formal Opening

Although already operating for several weeks, the Merry Garden held its formal opening on this day. Under the proprietorship of J. Paul Warrick, the Merry Garden offered sandwiches, fountain drinks, tobacco, patent medicines, magazines, Eastman Kodaks and film and other sundries. The establishment advertised that it especially catered to picnickers, furnishing excellent lunches for outings of that nature. They also served chicken dinners each Sunday. The building, located on Broad Street, was constructed by local general contractors Jones and Wexler.

September 16, 1955

Stop Sign Stabbing

The preliminary hearing of an Eastman foreman and his wife, charged with the stabbing attack of a motorist who ran a stop sign, began today. Effend and Deba Barrett were accused of violently attacking Earl Jones, who testified he suffered slashes on his arm, chest and groin. His injuries required over one hundred stiches. Prior to the altercation, Jones ran a stop sign at the intersection of Poplar and East Sevier Streets. The Barrettes stopped Jones, who then apologized for running the stop sign, but evidently the situation escalated, with Jones being injured. The stop sign in question was only a few months old, and Jones claimed he didn't see it.

September 17, 1946

"Kingsport Day"

This day was designated "Kingsport Day" at the Washington County Fair in Gray's Station. Kingsport citizens and civic leaders alike were expected to make this year's attendance the biggest crowd in the history of the fair. Kingsport citizens would be the first to see the fair, when perishable displays were the freshest and the entertainment had that extra spark of newness. Johnson City Day would be Thursday, and Friday was "school day." Free attractions were scheduled for each afternoon of the fair. Fair officials noted that everything from pigs to pears and potatoes would be rated by judges. Perishables were to be judged Wednesday and livestock on Thursday.

September 18, 1918

The Central School Building

On this day, the new Central School Building for Kingsport Public Schools opened. The school was the first public school opened since the incorporation of Kingsport in March 1917. Open to students of grades first through twelfth, the Central School later became the first George Washington Elementary School. The school building was remodeled and is the present-day site of the George Washington School Apartments.

September 19, 2015

Charles Wright

Students of East Tennessee State University's English honor society, Sigma Tau Delta, gathered on this day at the Kingsport Public Library and Archives to dedicate a marker in honor of Charles Wright. The dedication included a reading of Wright's Kingsport poems. Wright, born in Pickwick Dam, Tennessee, spent his formative years in Kingsport. A former poet laureate of the United States, Charles Wright is often ranked as one of the best American poets of his generation. Wright garnered a lot of attention with his collection of works and has won numerous awards, including the Pulitzer Prize, the Griffin International Poetry Prize and a Ruth Lilly Poetry Prize.

September 20, 1965

Ben Haden

The Reverend Ben Haden, former Kingsport businessman and news publisher and pastor of the Key Biscayne Presbyterian Church in Miami, conducted services on this day at the First Presbyterian Church. Haden would be conducting services for several days at the church. During the week, Haden also spoke to the Kingsport Kiwanis Club. Before Haden entered the ministry, he earned a degree from the University of Texas and a law degree from Washington and Lee. Reverend Ben Haden would go on to become a distinguished author and founder of the ministry Changed Lives.

September 21, 1949

Hearings Started

Judge Shelburne Ferguson started hearings on circuit court dockets composed of 1,545 cases this afternoon. The morning court sessions were spent in selection of the grand and petit juries. Judge Ferguson, in his charge to the grand jury, reminded the jurors of the importance of the panel in protecting the homefront while soldiers from this county were helping to safeguard the nation's freedom. Selection of the jury was difficult, as nearly every farmer asked to be excused. According to A.N. Hawk, circuit court clerk, more people asked to be relieved of jury duty than ever before. Farmers were having a difficult time employing workers, and many were being forced to harvest their crops with very little, if any, help.

SEPTEMBER 22, 1955

Elvis at Civic Auditorium

Elvis Presley played his first and only show in Kingsport on this day, at the Civic Auditorium, promoted by WKIN. Elvis was traveling with the Cowboy Copas and the Louvin Brothers and was billed as the middle act. Elvis and his band stayed at the Brickey Hotel on Memorial Boulevard. He opened his set with "Rock Around the Clock" and ended it with "I Love You Because" to a crowd of fewer than three hundred people.

SEPTEMBER 23, 1956

Dr. T.B. Yancey

The *Kingsport Times-News* reported the death of Dr. Thomas Bragg Yancey. Yancey, a veteran Kingsport physician, came to Kingsport in 1916 to set up the first Public Health Unit. In 1925, Yancey set up a general practice and later served as the resident physician at Holston Valley Community Hospital for many years. As resident physician, Yancey remained at the hospital both day and night, catching sleep when he could in between calls. He served as president of the Sullivan County Board of Health, was a member of the State Board of Medical Examiners and was first staff chairman of the Holston Valley Community Hospital. In 1948, he married Mamie Dugger, RN, then a member of the hospital staff. He was survived by Mrs. Yancey, one son and four daughters. The funeral service was held at St. Paul's Episcopal Church.

SEPTEMBER 24, 2010

V.O. Dobbins Sr. Complex

Kingsport City leaders were on hand for a ribbon-cutting and dedication of the V.O. Dobbins Sr. Community Complex. The $8.2 million project highlights the efforts of the community to rejuvenate the Riverview

Community and honor an influential member of the community. V.O. Dobbins was the third and last principal of Douglass School, from 1942 to 1966. A state historic marker denoting the structure's original usage as the former Douglass High School was also unveiled. After extensive renovation and expansion, the V.O. Dobbins Sr. Complex is home to Head Start, nonprofit agencies, several community health resources and the Sons and Daughters of Douglass Alumni Association.

September 25, 1963

Kidnapping Charges Dismissed

Charges of kidnapping against Mary Hamblen for allegedly detaining another woman's husband were dismissed by Judge Walter Moody. Hamblin had been charged by Mrs. Whittamore with unlawfully detaining her husband, R.C. Whittamore. In court on this day, Mrs. Whittamore took the stand without an attorney to give her testimony against Hamblen and to give her opinion that the case be dismissed. Judge Moody, in dismissing the charges, reprimanded Mrs. Whittamore for the "scandalous" way in which she had charges levied against another woman when she (Mrs. Whittamore) could not control her husband.

September 26, 1940

Hog Cholera

Kingsport city health officials gave reports today that Kingsport was in the midst of a serious hog cholera epidemic. A warning was issued against the purchase of pork from sources that had not been inspected and approved for food purposes. The epidemic was rampant in Long Island, Highland Park and sections north of the city near the Virginia border. Veterinarian and city food inspector Dr. J.F. Kagey cautioned residents not to buy meat that had not been inspected and stamped. The epidemic was attributed to the failure of hog raisers to vaccinate their stock at the proper times.

September 27, 1947

Teen Center

Construction on the new Kingsport Teen Center had started, and progress was coming along nicely. Mayor Gene Armitage was present to lay the first brick for the center. The Teen Center was a Junior Chamber of Commerce Youth Project. The building was slated to be fireproof and of modern design. The building would also be equipped for showing movies and have an auditorium and stage, a game room with table tennis and a completely modern soda fountain. It was hoped that the formal opening of the building would be around the holidays. Hoping to offset some of the costs for the center, the Junior Chamber of Commerce partnered with the American Legion to host a teen carnival, with the all proceeds going toward construction of the building.

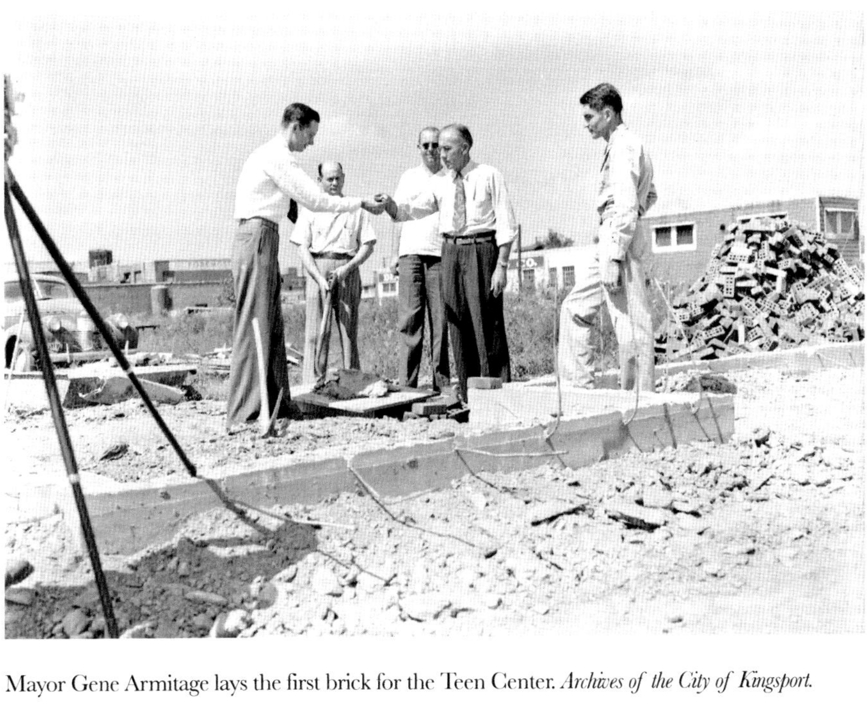

Mayor Gene Armitage lays the first brick for the Teen Center. *Archives of the City of Kingsport.*

September 28, 1940

"Kingsport Days"

This day marked the third and final day of "Kingsport Days." "Kingsport Days" offered great sales and encouraged visitors from all over the region to shop in Kingsport. According to Henry Lipman, member of the "Kingsport Days" publicity committee, the campaign of "Kingsport has it" caught on with shoppers in Virginia in particular. The lower fares offered by the Clinchfield Railroad proved to be advantageous in attracting visitors.

September 29, 1955

PET Dairy Grand Opening on Konnarock Road

The dairy plant on Konnarock Road held its grand opening and open house to the public at 4:00 p.m. The plant had previously been located on the corner of West Market and Clay Streets since its formal opening in

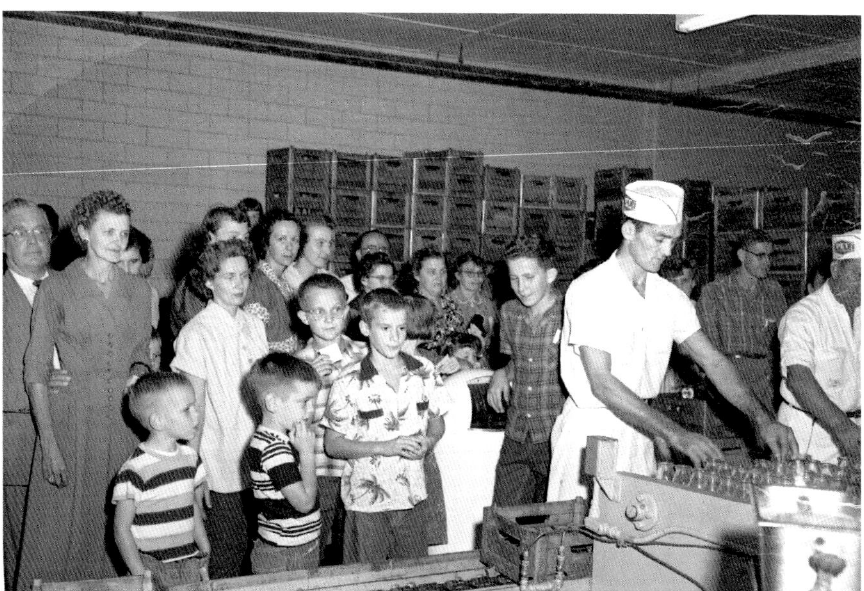

Visitors tour the PET Dairy Plant on Konnarock Road. *Archives of the City of Kingsport.*

September 1930. People were invited to the grand opening of the new plant, where they could tour the facilities and watch demonstrations by workers. Visitors were also invited to try samples of PET products, including Pet Brown Mule Ice Cream. The PET Dairy Plant on Konnarock Road was in operation until 2009.

September 30, 1923

Hobart Versus Hobart

Hobart White, a Kingsport youth of about nineteen, was admitted to the Riverview Hospital after being stabbed by Hobart Pruner. Pruner, who disappeared immediately after the stabbing, was being sought by police. The stabbing was said to be the result of a quarrel among the young men, who were returning home from attending a religious meeting at the Dale Street Tabernacle. Dr. E.W. Tipton listed White's condition as "reasonably favorable," and he was expected to make a full recovery. Pruner was discovered in Kermit, Virginia, where he was arrested and brought back to Kingsport and jailed. Charges were later dismissed, and Pruner was released after the court decided the evidence presented did not warrant a conviction.

OCTOBER

October 1, 1948

Freedom Train

From 1947 to 1949, the Freedom Train traveled all over the country carrying 127 documents and artifacts of historical significance to the United States. This was the first and only time that all of these documents and artifacts were assembled for public display. The Freedom Train toured the

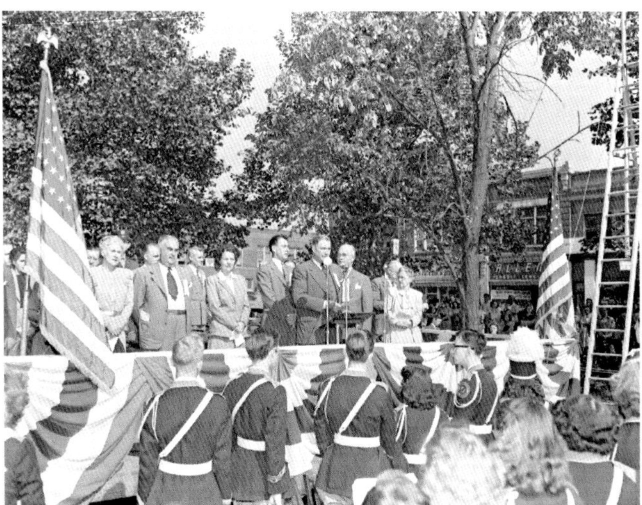

Freedom Train, scene of speeches and crowd. *Archives of the City of Kingsport.*

contiguous forty-eight states with the goal of "reawakening Americans to…the principles of liberty." The train allowed people to view documents such as the Constitution, the Declaration of Independence, Lincoln's Emancipation Proclamation and the Gettysburg Address. The "Freedom Documents" were guarded by the U.S. Marine Corps. The Freedom Train arrived at Kingsport's Clinchfield Railroad Station on this day in 1948. It was estimated that over eleven thousand people toured the train during its stop in Kingsport.

October 2, 1933

G-Men in Kingsport

Government agents descended on Kingsport today and arrested eight people on serious federal charges. Three of those arrested were accused of white slavery, or violating the Mann Act: Mark Frazier, Frazier's wife and his son, Pat Frazier. The elder Frazier was a former police officer and at the time was proprietor of the Tavern. The others arrested were being held as material witnesses against the accused. Several of the arrested confessed they were brought to Tennessee for immoral purposes. Seven federal agents, including one woman, conducted the raid unannounced, and it was the first undertaking in this country by the federal government in seeking to eliminate sex crimes.

October 3, 1925

Dobyns-Taylor Corn Show

A total of 850 exhibits of corn grown in Hawkins, Sullivan, Greene and Washington Counties were on display at the Dobyns-Taylor Hardware Company's corn show. The parkways on Broad Street from Market to Main Streets were lined with specially built tables on which the corn was displayed. F.L. Cloud delivered the address of welcome for the corn show. Music was provided by a ten-piece orchestra, and free movies about farm life were shown at the Strand Theatre to standing-room-only crowds. J.C. McAmis, state crop specialist, and H.P. Bird, county demonstrator, acted as the judges. Seven prizes were awarded. The winners were as follows: James Bayer, first place; J.D. McCraken, second place; Mrs. Cora Yarnes, third place; L.B. Christian, fourth place; C.L. Jones, fifth place; John Crawford, sixth place; and E.C. Smith, seventh place.

October 4, 1960

Aniline Plant Explosion

At 4:45 p.m., Kingsport was rocked by tragedy when the Eastman Aniline Plant Explosion occurred. The blast was felt all around the city, and even buildings downtown, over a mile away, were damaged. The explosion sent up a plume of black smoke that could be seen for miles. Residential homes in the area received damage, and debris from the explosion was found throughout the area. The blast rocked Eastman and the Kingsport community alike. Emergency crews raced to the scene from across eastern Tennessee and southwestern Virginia, and Holston

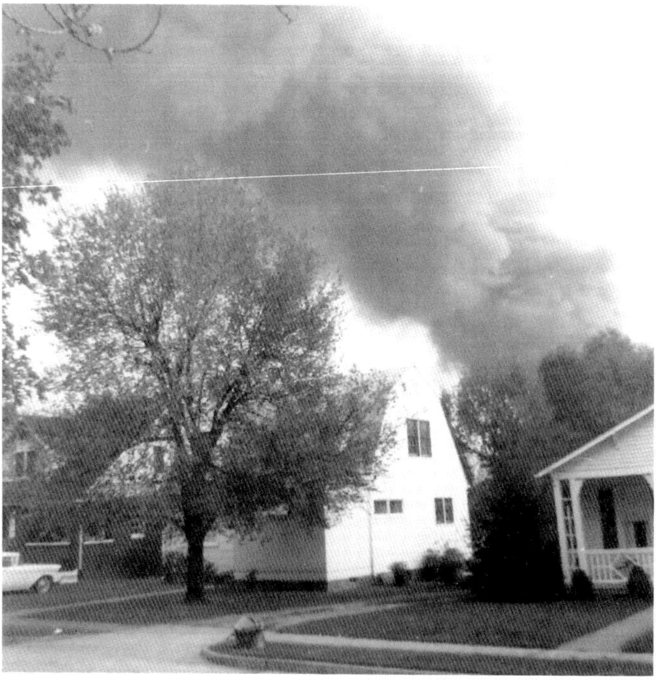

The plume of smoke from the Aniline Plant explosion. *Archives of the City of Kingsport.*

Valley Hospital prepared for the worst. The explosion remains the worst tragedy ever experienced in Kingsport. The death toll reached sixteen, and over two hundred were injured.

October 5, 1944

City Pays Tribute

Funeral services for the "Father of Kingsport," J. Fred Johnson, happened on this day at the First Presbyterian Church on Church Circle. Beginning at 2:00 p.m., all general stores closed down so employees could attend the funeral. The body of Johnson, one of Kingsport's first citizens, was to lie in state for most of the day before the services. Governor Prentice Cooper suggested that "there has never been a grander man than J. Fred Johnson. As the maker and builder of Kingsport, he left a monument that will do him honor forever." Evidence of Johnson's legacy can still be seen in Kingsport. The J. Fred Johnson Stadium, J. Fred Johnson Park and the J. Fred Johnson Memorial Library Building all bear his name.

October 6, 1918

Sergeant Hagan Hammond

Hagan Hammond, nineteen, son of Mr. and Mrs. J.M. Hammond of Chestnut Drive, was killed in action in Estrées, France. Hammond was the first from Sullivan County to be killed in World War I. Sergeant Hammond enlisted in the 117th Infantry in the early days of the war and was among the first troops to be sent overseas. The American Legion Hammond Post No. 3, the Hammond Bridge, Hammond Park and Hammond Avenue in Kingsport were all named in his honor and serve as a lasting tribute to him and the sacrifice he made for our country.

October 7, 1919

Whiskey in Hot Water Bottle

A Kingsport man was arrested by Patrolmen Moody and Parrott at a local boardinghouse. The man was arrested for having illicit whiskey that he had hidden in a hot water bottle, but he was soon out on a bail of fifty-five dollars. His charges included transporting whiskey in his hot water bottle, which incidentally was guaranteed not to spill. The water bottle was confiscated and placed in the city's safe deposit vault. Reports suggested there was little more than a quart in the bottle.

October 8, 1958

Nash Rambler

The new 1959 Nash Rambler went on sale today in Kingsport at Heck Motors. Customers could choose from the Six or Rambler Rebel V-8 models. The Rambler featured new exterior and interior styling and engineering changes designed to increase the economy of operation and durability. Heck Motors, on Center Street, was owned and operated by Raymond Heck. Opened in 1953, the original location was in Heck's garage on Clay Street. Heck Motors carried a complete line of Nash automobiles, station wagons and parts. Heck worked several years as a mechanic and service manager with the Nash agency run by Rass Morelock. Morelock closed his shop in 1951, leaving Kingsport without an authorized Nash dealership until Heck Motors opened.

October 9, 1938

Girls' Home

Thomas Williams of the City Mission announced today that work would continue this week on a building that would become a sanctuary for the unfortunate girls of Kingsport. The building, being remodeled both as a home for unfortunate girls and the City Mission, was located on Sullivan Street. The building was formerly home to Five Points Sheet and Metal Works. According to Mr. Williams, "Kingsport is in a real need for a refuge for those who have unwittingly been enmeshed in a web woven by lustful humanity….it is the aim of the mission to care for these unfortunate girls during their time of their greatest need and afterward to rehabilitate them and return them to the community as normal Christian girls, who profiting by their first lesson will be able to avoid future pitfalls."

October 10, 1976

Herbert G. Stone

Herbert G. Stone died on this day. Stone, credited with directing the development of the explosive RDX while heading a team of Tennessee Eastman scientists, died following a long illness. At the time of his death, he lived at Rotherwood Mansion. A native of Marion, Virginia, Stone came to Kingsport with the Federal Dyestuff and Chemical Corporation. In 1927, he began work at Tennessee Eastman. Under Stone's direction, the development of RDX led to the opening of Holston Ordnance Works, where he was employed as works manager. Following the war, Stone was presented the President's Certificate, then the highest civilian award for work in the National Defense Program. Stone was promoted to vice-president of Eastman in 1947 and remained in that position until his retirement. He was survived by his wife, Marguerite.

October 11, 1924

Bertram H. Borden

The mayor of Kingsport, J.W. Harrison, issued a proclamation that this day be a holiday and urged that all activities and usual business should be ceased. The reason for the holiday was the visit to the city by Bertram Borden, president of Borden Mill. Borden, who had recently decided to locate Borden Mill in Kingsport, was to be in town to lay the cornerstone of the first unit of the mill that was to be built. Governor Austin Peay was also going to be in Kingsport to welcome Borden. Citizens of Kingsport were urged to decorate their homes with flags and buntings. The whole city, including 1,800 students of Kingsport Public Schools marching in a parade, was expected to welcome the new industry and its dignitaries.

October 12, 1921

Holston Golf League Tournament

The first annual tournament of the recently organized Holston Golf League was held at the golf course of the Kingsport Country Club. The tournament also marked the formal opening of Kingsport's new golf course. The Holston Golf League comprised country clubs from Morristown, Johnson City, Greeneville, Bristol, Kingsport and Big Stone Gap. Maurice McCarthy, golf expert in charge of the grounds and builder of the course, noted that the local golf course had a reputation of being one of the longest in the country. The golf course was designed by A.W. Tillinghast, one of the most prolific golf course architects. Tillinghast designed the course to be interesting to both experts and beginners of the game. The course was laid out on 135 acres and designed to be 6,700 yards long, 300 yards longer than a championship course.

October 13, 1929

The First American Legion Carnival

The first American Legion Carnival kicked off its week of fun with general chairman C.P. Edwards Jr. remarking, "She is all set." The carnival officially opened to the public on the following day. The carnival was financed by the American Legion Hammond Post No. 3 and would be managed throughout the week by Kingsport legionnaires. Throughout the week there would be games, shows, contests, miniature golf, boxing fights, carnival food, special attractions and just about anything you could

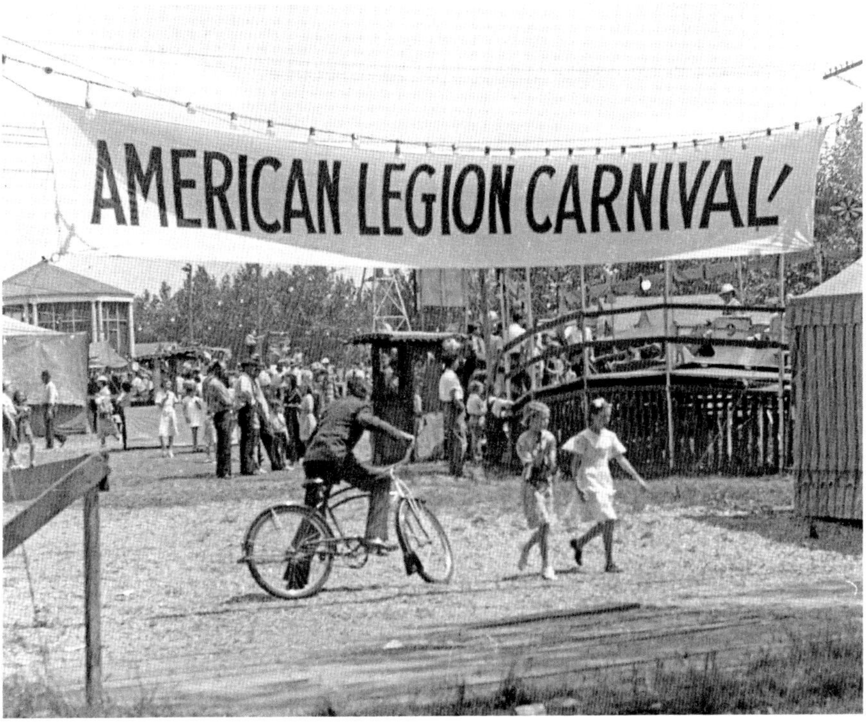

American Legion Carnival. *Archives of the City of Kingsport.*

imagine. Each night featured two death-defying acts with Captain Hugo, daredevil cyclist and high diver. The carnival became one of the most highly anticipated events of the summertime.

October 14, 1944

Kingsport Business and Professional Women's Club

This day marked the climax of the Kingsport Business and Professional Women's Club's celebration of National Business Women's Week. The group held a tea at the home of Mrs. Hubert A. Quillen on Sevier Street. The National Foundation of Business and Professional Women was formed in 1919 as a response to the number of women needed in the workforce during World War I. Some goals of the organization included providing resources for and about working women and securing equal pay and working conditions for women. The Kingsport chapter supported the programs of the national organization, worked to increase knowledge of community services and opportunities and participated in projects that helped women and children.

October 15, 2009

Dobyns-Bennett High School Alumni Hall of Fame

The first annual induction ceremony for the Dobyns-Bennett High School Alumni Hall of Fame was held on this day. Five alumni were inducted in the first class of hall of famers. The inaugural inductees were Robert Lee "Bobby" Dodd, John R. "Jack" King, Fred "Pal" Barger, Kenneth W. "Ken" Simonds and Dr. Jack McConnell. The Alumni Hall of Fame was created to recognize and honor the accomplishments and contributions of Dobyns-Bennett High School graduates and/or teachers and administrators who had a profound effect on Dobyns-Bennett High School and the community. Nomination categories for Dobyns-Bennett Graduates include academics, administrator/teacher, arts, athletics, business, church and ministerial, entertainment, government services/humanitarian, judicial and legal, literature, medical, military service, news and communications (media), politics, public service and science. Nomination categories for nongraduates of Dobyns-Bennett include administrators, teachers, staff and friends.

October 16, 1954

Oakwood Market Robbery

Two masked men held up the Oakwood Market on West Sullivan Street near the store's closing time. The robbers got away with around $12,300. The men, wearing nylon stockings over their faces, walked into the store, and one man yelled, "This is a stickup! Hit the floor or I will shoot your g— d— hearts out!" While one of the men held about a dozen people at gunpoint, the other went to the business office to get the money. The men managed to get away before police arrived. Oakwood Market, a highly successful local

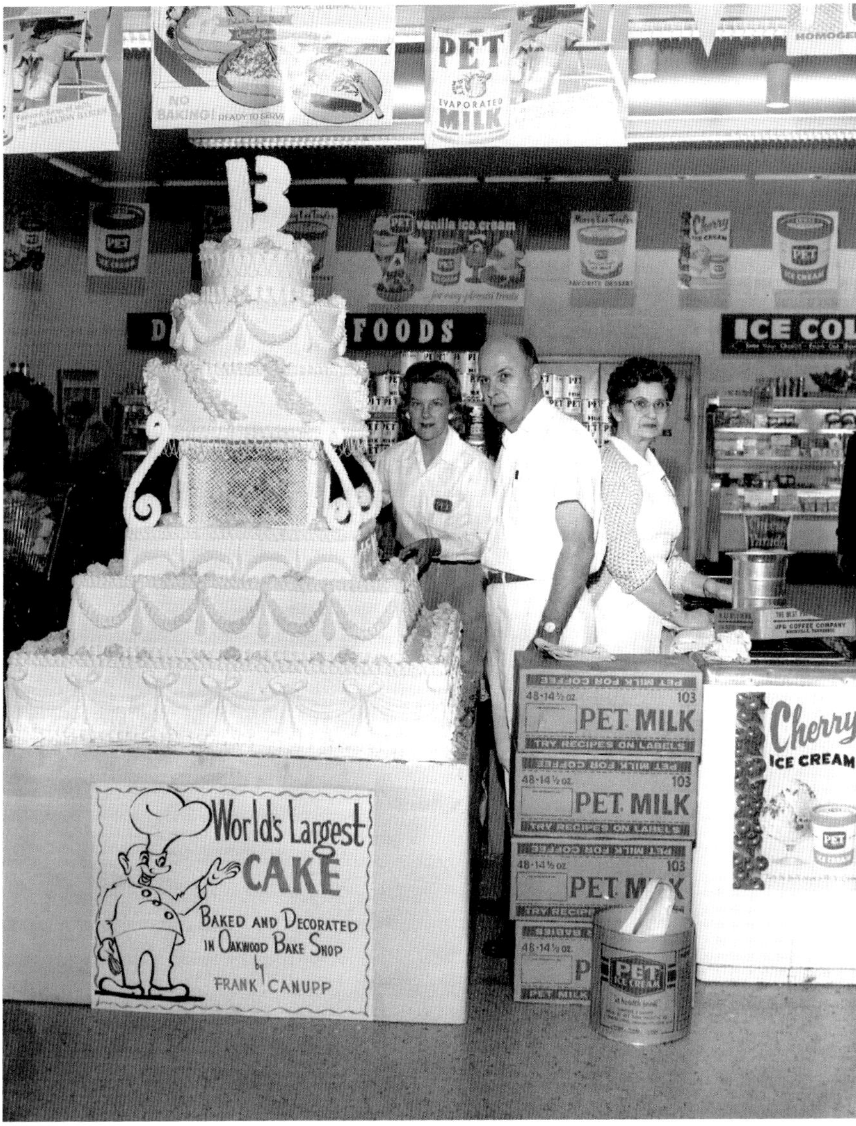

Oakwood Market, thirteenth anniversary cake. *Archives of the City of Kingsport.*

grocery store, was opened in 1947 on Eastman Road. The West Sullivan Street location opened in 1950 and was the first store to occupy what later became Supermarket Row.

October 17, 1924

Rotary Club

The Rotary Club of Kingsport was officially organized on this day at a meeting at the Kingsport Inn. The club began with an initial membership of twenty-five, the maximum allowed by Rotary laws. More than that amount signed up as members. They continued to sign up as rapidly as possible. The Rotary laws state that only three new members can be taken in a month. The board of directors chosen consisted of J. Fred Johnson, J.H. Thickens, O.S. Hauk, B.M. Brown, L.M. Fuller, J.B. Nall and J.E. Huffaker. Dr. O.S. Hauk was elected the first president of the club. Several representatives of the Rotary Club of Johnson City were on hand to assist in the organizing of the club. It was decided that the club would meet for luncheons on Wednesdays each week at noon, with the meeting place determined at the meeting prior.

October 18, 1947

Tropical Garden

The Tropical Garden held its formal opening on this day. The store was located on the Bristol Highway (now East Center Street) near the intersection of Dale Street. The business was a glorified roadside fruit stand, complete

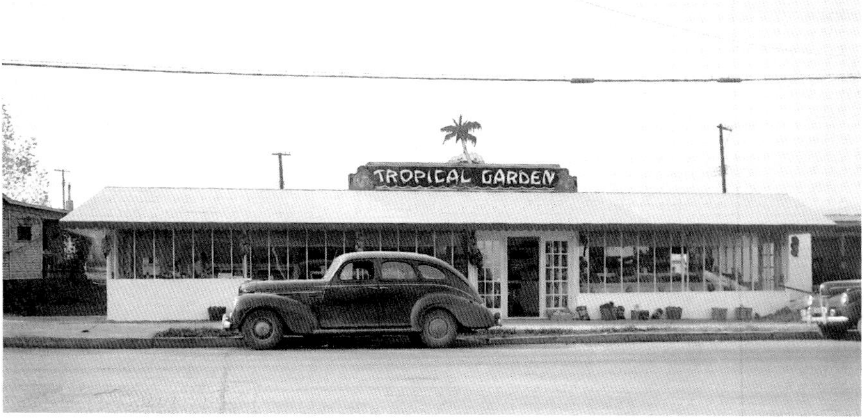

The Tropical Garden, East Center Street. *Archives of the City of Kingsport.*

with a full line of groceries and a soda fountain. The Tropical Garden featured fresh fruits that were brought by truck from Florida twice a week. They advertised bringing fresh fruits and vegetables to the housewives of Kingsport. The Tropical Garden carried a lot of local brands like Foremost Milk, Southern Maid and Holsum Bread. Within a few years, the Tropical Garden became known as the Tropical Garden Bar and Delicatessen.

October 19, 1948

Industrial Exposition

Over eight thousand people were in attendance at the Industrial Exposition sponsored by the Kingsport Rotary Club. The industrial exposition was deemed a great success, as the first two days alone brought twelve thousand visitors to check out the varied exhibits. The biggest crowd surrounded the fashion exhibitions sponsored by Tennessee Eastman and the Borden

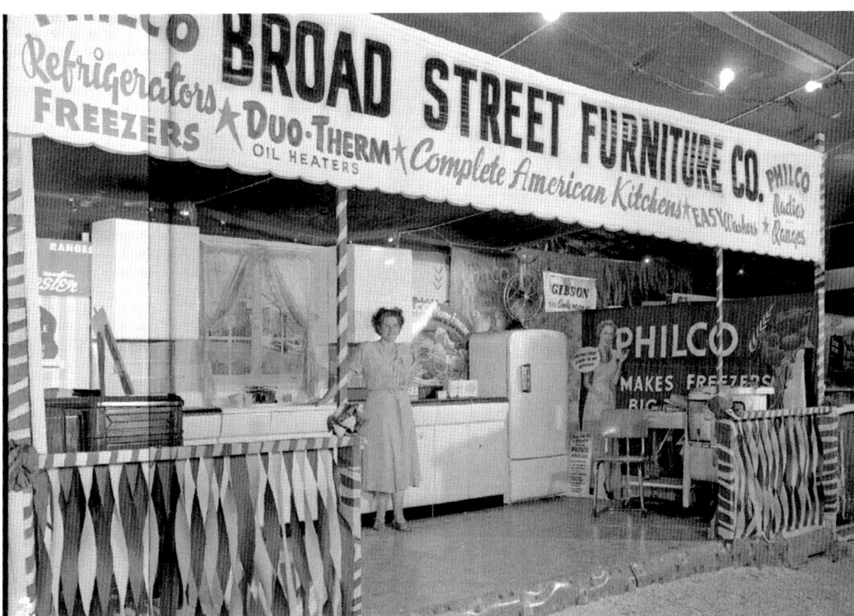

Broad Street Furniture booth at the Rotary Club Expo. *Archives of the City of Kingsport.*

Mill exhibit, which featured an exhibition of high-speed dress making. The finished product was raffled off. The Industrial Exposition featured a glimpse into most of the major industrial plants and a variety of businesses throughout the Tri-Cities.

October 20, 1970

Nixon Visits the Tri-Cities

A crowd of over eight thousand waited in the on again, off again rain at the Tri-Cities Airport to greet President Richard Nixon. Accompanying Nixon was Republican gubernatorial candidate Winfield Dunn and Senate hopeful Bill Brock. Nixon was scheduled to arrive at the Tri-Cities Airport and immediately be taken to East Tennessee State University in Johnson City. The crowd at East Tennessee State University was estimated at fifty thousand. This was Nixon's second trip to Tennessee that year. In May, he appeared at the Billy Graham Crusade at the University of Tennessee in Knoxville.

October 21, 1969

Fuzz Pills

Mrs. Don Johnson of Cloud Apartments testified on this day in general sessions court that she did shoot her husband and that "fuzz" pills were to blame for the problems between them. According to Mrs. Johnson, on the day her husband was killed, he was "half-drunk" on pills and threatened to kill her unborn baby by hitting her in the stomach with the radio. Mrs. Johnson told him she would kill him if he harmed her baby, to which he replied, "I don't think you have the guts." Loading the shotgun, she pointed it at him. When he tried to grab it, she pulled the trigger. She put the shotgun down and immediately went out to tell her neighbor that she had just killed her husband. She also testified that whenever he was on pills, he would beat her and her kids. She was bound over under a $5,000 bond.

October 22, 1927

Don't Lend Your Tools

The Kingsport Police Department advised citizens to not lend their tools to strangers. The warning was issued after a serial "borrower" was released from jail. The so-called borrower had been held but was not charged because most of the people he borrowed from declined to press charges. The man had been asking to borrow stuff all over town but had yet to return anything. Handsaws, water hoses, hammers and other tools had all been taken with the same claim that he was working on a house nearby. After his release, the police department received more complaints about the man. It was noted that if the items were not returned, the man would this time be charged with fraudulent breach of trust.

October 23, 1982

The Strand Theatre Closes

The Strand Theatre officially closed its doors on this day. The first movie theater in Kingsport, it was originally located on the corner of Main and Shelby Streets and then moved to 140 Broad Street (former home of Goodwin Furniture Company) in 1925. The building on the corner of Main and Shelby later became the Gem Theatre. In 1989, the Restoration Church moved into the historic theater building. Then, the theater was purchased from the Restoration Church and became the new home of the Lamplight Theater in May 2013. The building has undergone an extensive renovation.

October 24, 1976

Former Mayor Dead

The *Kingsport Times* announced the death of former Kingsport mayor Fred Gillette, who served the city from 1969 to 1971. He also served eight years on the BMA, three of those as vice-mayor. Gillette was past president of the Kingsport Chamber of Commerce, past president of the Merchants Bureau and past vice-president of the East Tennessee Retail Furniture Association. Born in Greene County, Tennessee, he often told the story of how he hitched a ride to Kingsport with only nine dollars in his pocket. Standing on Main Street, he said to himself, "Someday, I'm going to be mayor of this town."

October 25, 1944

WCTU Convention

The state convention of the Woman's Christian Temperance Union (WCTU) was held in Kingsport on this day. The convention opened at 10:00 a.m. with state president Mrs. Winnie Welsh presiding. Mrs. George Woodward was president of the Kingsport chapter of the WCTU at the time, and Mrs. J.M. Cross served as district chairman for more than twenty years. Other officers from the Kingsport chapter include Mrs. W.L. Lauderback (treasurer), Mrs. L.R. Richmond (chairman of convention) and Mrs. R.S. Showkier (finance chairman and entertainment, publicity and evangelistic chairman). Special music was provided by Mrs. Broughton Hutchins.

October 26, 1931

Poison Drinker

Ruth Hendrickson, a fifteen-year-old high school girl, attempted suicide this evening by drinking a pint of Lysol at her home in the Litz-Manor Addition. Ruth Hendrickson left a goodbye note for her parents telling them she wanted to end it all. According to her parents, the girl had been despondent for several days prior, but they could not think of a motive. After dinner, the girl retreated to her room and drank the Lysol. Mrs. Walter B. Hendrickson was alerted to the situation by screams of pain coming from the girl's bedroom. Mrs. Hendrickson said the girl had a nervous breakdown at a school dance and was taken out of school. She had returned only recently, but her mother said she was becoming more and more nervous each day. Ruth was unconscious when she was admitted to the hospital, and her prospects of recovery were unknown.

October 27, 1964

Barry Goldwater

Over twenty-five thousand spectators were at the Tri-Cities Airport to see and hear Republican senator Barry Goldwater. Goldwater delivered the hardest-hitting attacks on the Johnson administration and called the greeting one of the largest he had encountered in his eight weeks of campaigning. Goldwater was introduced by First District representative James "Jimmy" H. Quillen. His visit to the Tri-Cities marked the first stop in his last week of campaigning. Goldwater, a five-term U.S. Senator from Arizona, was the Republican Party's nominee for president in the 1964 election. He was a major general in the U.S. Air Force Reserve and known as "Mr. Conservative."

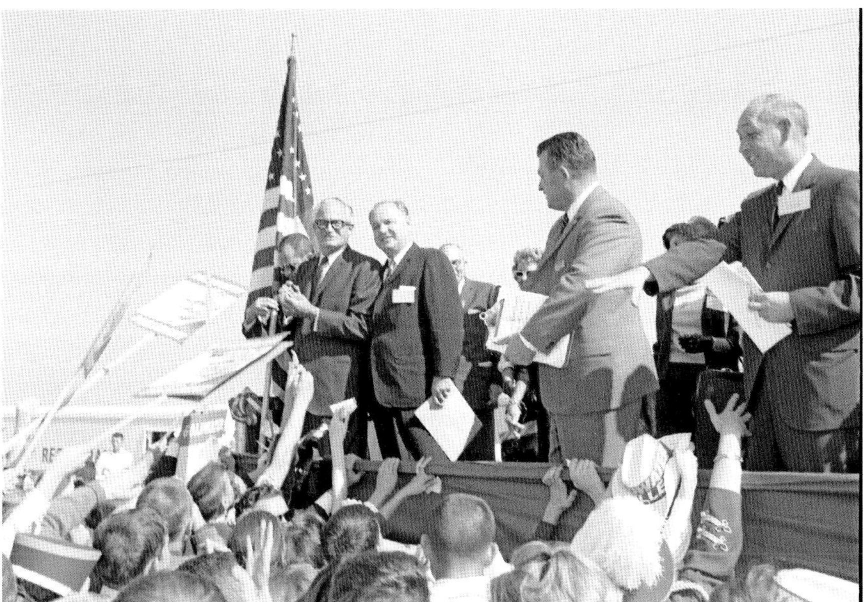

Barry Goldwater and Jimmy Quillen at Goldwater's campaign stop at the Tri-Cities Airport. *Archives of the City of Kingsport.*

October 28, 1931

Pumpkin Club

More than four thousand farmers and their families were in Kingsport on this day for the Pumpkin Club Program sponsored by Dobyns-Taylor Hardware Company. Pumpkins of all shapes, sizes and varieties were lined up on display on Broad Street from Church Circle to Main Street. Prizes will be awarded for the biggest pumpkin, the best pumpkin and the freak pumpkin. In early spring of this year, Dobyns-Taylor gave pumpkin seeds to farmers in Sullivan, Washington, Greene, Hancock and Hawkins Counties, Tennessee, and Scott County, Virginia, with the stipulation that they would participate in the pumpkin-growing contest.

October 29, 2013

Eastman Expansion

Many people gathered on this day to watch officials break ground for Eastman Chemical Company's new company headquarters in Kingsport. "This city wants to say thank you for ensuring the corporate headquarters of the Eastman Chemical Company remains in Kingsport, Tennessee. It's a great day," said Kingsport mayor Dennis Phillips. The new headquarters was expected to bring more than three hundred jobs to the area within the next few years. Eastman's Kingsport location was opened in 1920.

October 30, 1949

Fordtown Girl Killed

A twenty-five-year-old Fordtown girl on her way home from church was killed when her car was hit by a diesel-drawn Clinchfield freight train at the Fordtown grade crossing. Sarah Geneva Houser was the daughter of

Mr. and Mrs. Millard Houser, and her companion, Laurence Millhourn, sustained serious injuries in the accident. Both victims were thrown from the car, and Houser's body was found some sixty feet from the railroad crossing. There were no signals on the crossing where the accident occurred. Witnesses reported that Millhourn, who was driving, must have seen the train as he was crossing the tracks because it looked like he tried to back up before the engine hit.

October 31, 1930

Halloween Party

Dr. and Mrs. Will Hutchins hosted a Halloween party at their home on the Bristol Highway. The party was to be an old-fashioned, southern Halloween party. Invitations were extended to the Rotary Club, Kiwanis Club and the American Legion. Guests were encouraged to wear appropriate Halloween costumes. The party featured a candy pulling and included music, old-time fiddling and an opossum hunt. A flower show was held in conjunction with the Halloween party. A dozen roses were to be presented to the lady rendering the best modern music on violin.

NOVEMBER

November 1, 1954

Polio Vaccine Testing

It was announced on this day that the final phase of polio testing would be conducted on November 2. Blood samples would be taken at five Sullivan County schools, and children who gave blood for testing in the spring were expected to participate in the final testing. Kingsport city schools and some Sullivan County schools were selected as a test site for the polio vaccine, then the largest and most significant clinical trial in the history of medicine. Over twenty-four thousand schoolchildren in Sullivan County and Kingsport were inoculated during the first few days of field trials. In Sullivan County, only children in the second grade were vaccinated with the polio trial vaccine. In Kingsport, the vaccinations were given at Lincoln, Johnson, Washington, Lee and Jackson Schools. Each child was vaccinated by a physician, with registered nurses assisting. Children were given a total of three shots over a period of six weeks.

November 2, 2003

James "Jimmy" H. Quillen

James "Jimmy" H. Quillen died on this day. Quillen was a Republican member of the U.S. House of Representatives from Tennessee from 1963 to 1997. Quillen holds the record for the longest unbroken tenure of a Tennessean within the U.S. House of Representatives. Quillen, a Scott County, Virginia native, graduated from Dobyns-Bennett High School. In 1936, Quillen became the youngest publisher in the country when he began publishing the *Kingsport Mirror*. Quillen reportedly invested his own personal money to start the weekly paper. In 1939, he sold the paper and moved to Johnson City to start the *Johnson City Times*. Quillen eventually became a lieutenant in the U.S. Navy and began his foray into politics in 1954, when he was elected to the Tennessee House of Representatives. Quillen is buried in Kingsport's Oak Hill Cemetery.

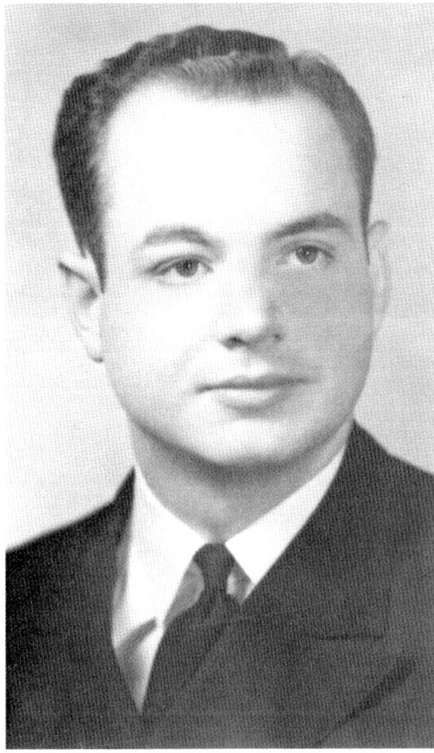

Portrait of Jimmy Quillen, circa 1934. *Archives of the City of Kingsport.*

November 3, 1935

Relief Workers

More than one hundred relief workers were hired to work on the construction of the Tri-Cities Airport project. The workers began the preliminary work on what was being called the most momentous project in the history of

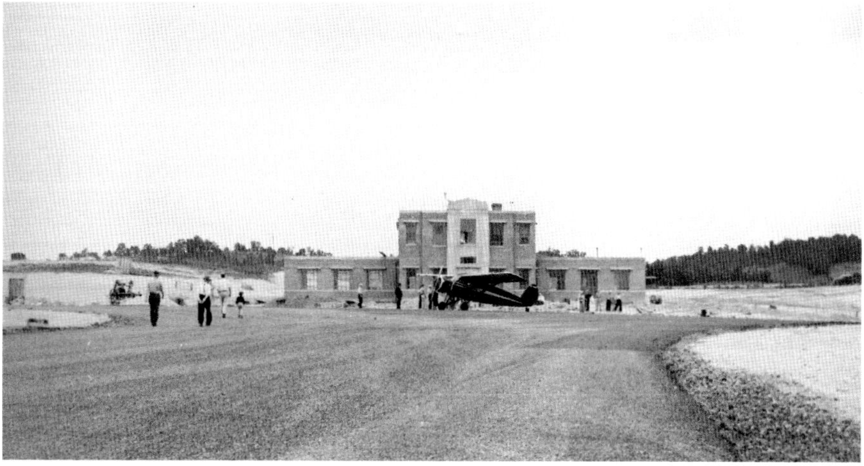

Tri-Cities Airport/McKellar Field. *Archives of the City of Kingsport.*

Sullivan County. After the preliminary work was finished and the site cleared, bids would be accepted immediately. F.L. St. John, former work supervisor of the Works Progress Administration at Greeneville, was transferred to the new project and in charge of the initial operation. When the actual construction started, more than four hundred relief workers would be on site. The Tri-Cities Airport project was a collaborative, cost-sharing effort by Johnson City, Bristol, Sullivan County and Kingsport. The goal was to build a regional airport that would serve the aviation needs of the area, as the smaller airfields in each city were no longer practical.

November 4, 1941

Preliminary Hearing for Clay Shipley

The *Kingsport Times* reported that the preliminary hearing for Clay Shipley, charged with murder in connection with the death of Ernest Whetsel, had been set. The preliminary hearing was to take place Friday before Judge George E. Bradley. Shipley was accused of shooting Whetsel in a fight, and he surrendered to authorities two hours after the shooting. Whetsel was a former business manager of Russell Brothers circus and a livestock dealer. Funeral services for Whetsel were held this afternoon at Solomon's Temple. Shipley's brother, Cleve, was also on trial and faced charges of assault and battery with intent to commit murder and aiding and abetting in murder. Cleve Shipley was later acquitted of the charges, and Clay Shipley, who pleaded self-defense, was found guilty of involuntary manslaughter and sentenced to two years in the state penitentiary.

November 5, 1925

Naming of Dobyns-Bennett High School

At a meeting of the Kingsport Board of Education, it was decided that the new high school building, currently under construction, would be named in honor of J.W. Dobyns and W.M. Bennett Sr. Dobyns and Bennett were two of Kingsport's most honored citizens and spent a major part of their lives in devoted service to the city. J.W. Dobyns was the first mayor of Kingsport, and W.M. Bennett Sr. was chairman of the first Board of Education. The Board of Education voted for the new school building to be named Dobyns-Bennett High School, and it opened in 1926 on Wateree Street. The building currently houses John Sevier Middle School.

November 6, 1956

Safe Stolen from Sullivan County High School

Roughly $3,000 in cash and checks was stolen out of a safe at Sullivan County High School. The five-hundred-plus-pound safe was taken from the cafeteria. Entry to the school was gained by breaking a window, and the door to the office was pried open. An investigation was underway and prints made of the tire tracks that were found near the scene. Chief investigator O.C. Akard said the safe was taken from the school by a light truck or car between midnight and daylight.

November 7, 1952

Clean Sweep

Police chief G.W. Fletcher warned that some Kingsport merchants may be fined or cited in court if they did not see to it that the sidewalks in front of their places were swept after closing time on Saturday nights. A city ordinance made businesses responsible for the cleanliness of the sidewalks in front of their buildings. The ordinance specified this must be done every weekday morning and at the close of business on Saturday. Chief Fletcher noted that last Sunday, police observed a number of littered sidewalks. The worst area was in the block of Cherokee between New and Sullivan Streets and some places on Main.

November 8, 1945

Douglass High Homecoming Game

The Douglass High School Tigers beat Marion 31–0 during their homecoming game held at J. Fred Johnson Park. The homecoming game hosted the largest crowd of the season. The Tigers kept the ball in enemy territory virtually the whole game, never letting Marion advance to the Douglass 40. Members of the team included Ralph Banner, Andy Watterson, D. Blye, Paul Horton, John Johnson, Robert Taylor, Vern Allen and Gray. Another highlight of the homecoming game was the half-time crowning of the year's Miss Douglass, Dorothy Ervin, a sophomore.

November 9, 1958

Dr. Tipton Dies

Dr. Tipton, prominent Kingsport physician, succumbed to a fatal heart attack on this day. Tipton was considered a city pioneer. Three years before Kingsport was chartered, he constructed the city's first business building, on the corner of Main and Broad Streets. He continued to operate from that building for over forty years. Dr. Tipton ranked among the city's civic leaders, and he served on the BMA and was once the mayor of Kingsport. He was a charter member of the Kingsport Kiwanis Club, a member of the Masonic Lodge No. 688 and a charter member of the First Presbyterian Church of Kingsport. Also a leader in business, he was vice-president and director of the First National Bank and of Kingsport Savings and Loan, former director of the Kingsport Broadcasting Company and former director of the Kingsport Publishing Company. He was survived by his widow, Mrs. Kate Nelms Tipton.

November 10, 1939

Highland Drug Opens

The formal opening of the Highland Drug Company, at its new location in the Francis-Cox building in Highland Park, occurred on this day. The building was owned by Dr. Paul Cox and P.G. Fields. The building housed the offices of two physicians, one dentist, a hosiery and lingerie shop, a beauty shop, an apartment and the drugstore. The drugstore and the beauty shop were owned and operated by Mr. Francis. The interior of the drugstore was equipped with open counters and display shelves, allowing customers to wait on themselves if they so desired.

November 11, 2015

Veterans Memorial

Hundreds converged in Kingsport to stand proudly as the city and community leaders dedicated the expansion of Kingsport's Veterans Memorial. Located in J. Fred Johnson Park along Fort Henry Drive, the city's memorial currently has six granite tablets recognizing 375 fallen soldiers from Kingsport. The walkways leading into the memorial include 1,728 granite pavers bearing the names of veterans from all conflicts. The new dedication focused on the addition of 392 pavers to add to the park, which is a location managed by Kingsport Parks and Recreation. Phase I of the

Veterans Memorial was dedicated in 2008. The Veterans Memorial began through a project with Kingsport Tomorrow. After Kingsport Tomorrow transitioned to an all-volunteer organization, the City of Kingsport took the lead on the project.

November 12, 2005

Scott Adams Memorial Skate Park

A Grand Opening Jam was held on this day for the Scott Adams Memorial Skate Park. The skate park, located in Frank Cloud Park, was dedicated to the memory of Scott Adams. Adams was thirteen when he was killed by a car while trying to retrieve his skateboard on Stone Drive. The idea of a skate park had been floating around for a while and led to Kingsport Tomorrow convening a task force. Funding, however, was an issue. After Adams's death, there was a renewed interesting in building a safe place for kids to skate. His parents, Jackie and Mike, led a grass-roots effort to build the park. The ten-thousand-square-foot skate park features two bowls (one twelve feet deep), steps and a grinding rail.

November 13, 1948

Teen Center Opens

The Teen Center officially opened its doors with a Sadie Hawkins Day Dance. The Jaycee-sponsored project held a recognition ceremony to pay tribute to the many people and businesses that assisted in the $40,000 project. The ceremony was broadcast on WKPT. An open house was held for the public to tour the center. Music for the occasion was provided by Sammie Devault and his orchestra, and prizes were awarded for the best dressed Sadie Hawkins Day characters. Admission for the event was free, but teens had the opportunity to sign up for membership for one dollar, which was the amount of dues for the first three months. After the membership drive, it was in the plans for the teens to operate the center themselves. All activities at the Teen Center would be adequately chaperoned.

November 14, 1923

Surprise Musical Performance

Local Rotarians at their regular weekly luncheon meeting at the Kingsport Inn were treated to a surprise musical performance by Augusta Riley and Helen Adams. Riley was the director of music for Kingsport Public Schools, and Adams was with Kingsport's Central High School. Riley sang a number of catchy musical selections, and Adams, accompanied by Riley on piano, played several selections on violin. Afterward, all of the Rotarians agreed that the program was one of the most enjoyable ones yet. Charles Harkader, vice-president of the Bristol Rotary Club, was also on hand to give fellow Rotarians a quick speech for the luncheon.

November 15, 1988

Coty Sensabaugh

Coty Sensabaugh was born on this day. A cousin of Gerald Sensabaugh, Coty is a professional football cornerback for the Los Angeles Rams. Sensabaugh is a graduate of Dobyns-Bennett High School. He played college football at Clemson University and was drafted by the Tennessee Titans in the fourth round of the 2012 NFL Draft. In 2016, Sensabaugh signed with the Los Angeles Rams. That same year, he and his fiancée, Dominique Jordan, asked that in lieu of traditional wedding presents, wedding guests and others donate shoes or money to Soles4Souls, a nonprofit organization whose primary objective is to provide shoes to those in need. The couple are also benefactors of the Sensabuagh Camp Classic, a football camp held in Kingsport for children ages six to twelve.

November 16, 1919

Kingsport from the Clouds

Scores of Kingsporters took a tour of the city in a Curtis biplane flown by pilot Lieutenant J.J.R. Weiss. Weiss made the stop in Kingsport to carry passengers only while on a journey to Florida for the winter. Charging fifteen dollars seemed like a steep price, but it was reported that everyone who took the flight thought it was worth the money. Dr. W.Y. Hutchins, Aubrey Pyle, William Roller, Jr., Mrs. Maher, S.W. Sharett, Miss Marie Seward, Harry Mallis, Will Pierce and "Peg" Jones were among those who made the flight.

November 17, 1949

Kiwanis Club

It was announced today that the Kingsport Kiwanis Club would be presenting a sizeable check to the Tri-City Palsy Center. Dr. Roy Howard, chairman of the Kiwanis Kids' Day Committee, made the presentation on Saturday afternoon during the athletic contests. Money for the center was raised from the proceeds of the freshman football game between the University of Tennessee and the University of Kentucky. Some of the money also came from income from the Kiwanis Kapers. Kingsport was one of three thousand cities across the country that observed Kids' Day, which began as an effort to focus attention on underprivileged children.

November 18, 1921

Boost Kingsport!

The motto of the speeches delivered this evening at a meeting held at the Community YMCA building was "Boost Kingsport!" The meeting, attended by upward of three hundred people, was to discuss the idea of a men's business club. The result of the meeting was the official organization of the Kingsport Men's Business Club. The meeting was called to order by

George Burbage, one of the principal promoters of the club. A.D. Brockman was chosen as president of the club, and S.K. Lindsay was appointed as a committee of one to draw up the bylaws for the organization, to be presented at the next meeting.

November 19, 1956

Lost Boys

The *Kingsport Times* reported that the two teenaged boys that had been reported missing in the Bays Mountain area had been found. Alfred Crymble and "Skipper" Calheart of Linville Street were reported missing when they failed to return home from a hike across Bays Mountain. The boys had taken the wrong road and became lost when darkness fell, but they were discovered just a few hours after being reported missing. They were found by Captain Frank Williamson of the Tennessee Highway Patrol and Karl G. Goerdel, a neighbor. Around twenty-five people, law enforcement officials and neighbors, joined in the search for the boys.

November 20, 1945

39ers Club Dance

Ted Burton of the 39ers Club announced today that Dean Hutson and his band would not be here on the twenty-sixth but would appear at a later date. He did announce that the Thanksgiving dance would be held as scheduled at the civic auditorium and would feature Barney Rapp and his New Englanders. Rosemary Moore was the featured vocalist. Advanced tickets were on sale at Freels Drug and the Palace Fruit and News. Servicemen in uniform would be admitted for half price.

November 21, 1957

Dr. Crook

Dr. Charles Samuel Crook was arrested by the FBI at this office on Center Street. He was charged with trying to extort $25,000 from a prominent Baltimore surgeon, Dr. Frank C. Marino. The complaint against Dr. Crook alleged he threatened to injure the surgeon if the money was not received. Crook made the call from Kingsport to Marino's home. Dr. Crook was a former resident of Baltimore and practiced medicine there in the 1920s. Dr. Crook is the son of the late J.W. Crook, owner of a chain of grocery stores. The elder Crook left an estate worth $900,000 when he died. Crook was released on his own $5,000 bond.

November 22, 1948

Roman Banquet

The Dobyns-Bennett High School Latin classes of Miss Grace Elmore hosted an authentic Roman banquet at the Civic Auditorium. All of the students and guests were dressed as various Roman characters. Lois Ann Dryden served as chairman of the costume committee. Helen Jepson, opera star, attended in her own costume, a Greek garment she wore in the opera *Thais*. Dr. B.L. Ullman, author of the Latin textbook used at Dobyns-Bennett High School, was present in costume along with his wife. Jim Hansen, photographer, and Ben Wickersham, journalist, were sent by *Look* magazine to do a feature on the event. Freshman Latin students acted as slaves and served the food to the guests. The highlight of the nine-course menu was a thirty-pound roasted pig, complete with an apple in its mouth.

November 23, 1964

Not Welcome Here

General session court judge Walter Moody ordered *Kingsport Times-News* reporter Bill Robertson out of the judge's office after telling him he wasn't "welcome here." Roberts had written a story for the paper several weeks ago that alleged Judge Moody had illegally sentenced a boy to reform school without notifying his parents. The boy's mother had told Robertson that she did not know her son had been arrested and was not notified until after he had been tried and sentenced. State law specified that a juvenile must have a parent or guardian present before any action could take place. Moody was on vacation at the time, and this was his first day back on the job. Moody informed Roberts that he was welcome in the courtroom and welcome to look at public records but that he was not allowed in the judge's private office.

November 24, 1921

Thanksgiving Services

A large crowd gathered at the First Baptist Church on Broad Street for the union Thanksgiving services. The auditorium was filled to its capacity. Reverend Dean Bond, pastor of the First Christian Church, delivered the sermon. Special music was furnished by the Baptist church's male quartet, composed of Reverend Ogle, Dr. Reed, Dr. Highsmith and Howard Clifford. Reverend Robert King read the scripture, Reverend Woodyard led the prayer and Reverend Ogle pronounced the benediction. An offering for the Community Hospital was taken.

November 25, 1945

Christmas Candlelight Service

The *Kingsport Times* announced that the Kingsport Music Club would sponsor a Christmas Candlelight Service at the Broad Street United

Methodist Church on December 2 at 5:00 p.m. The program featured Christmas carols and songs by the chorus. The Reverend D. Trigg James presented the "Story of Christ Child." The music club choir was under the direction of Mrs. W.S. George, with Mrs. Hazel Huntoon accompanying on the organ. Members of the chorus were Mrs. J.S. Limble, Mrs. W.B. Hutchins, Mrs. M.J. Morison, Mrs. C.E. Holyoke, Mrs. W.C. Hillhouse, Miss Ann Buckles, Mrs. J.D. White, Mrs. Karl Goerdel, Mrs. O.A. Jared, Mrs. Conley Early, Mrs. C.H. Penning, Mrs. A.D. Brockman, Mrs. Melvin Smith, Mrs. J.W Shuey, Miss Dorothy Ring, Melvin Johnson, W.W. Hufford, Paul Overbay, J.W. Richey, R.L. Reynolds, Elder Reynolds, Lawson Reams, W.E. Gift, Raleigh Hampton, Reverend T.P. Johnsonton, Walter E. Cox, L.W. Hurst, Carl Hultin Sr., Raymond Herring and Robert Hasek. The string ensemble was composed of Mrs. Max Y. Parker, Mrs. J.W. Campbell, Mrs. Glenn Pendleton and Mrs. Richard Bailey.

November 26, 1943

Santa Train

Santa's Special Railroad Car pulled into town on this day in 1943, marking the first Santa Train excursion. The night before, a delegation of Kingsport merchants, staff writers and photographers from the *Kingsport Times-News* joined Mr. L.H. Phetteplace, general manager of the Clinchfield Railroad Company, in Kingsport to journey to Elkhorn City, Kentucky. It was from there that the delegation met up with Santa Claus and escorted him to Kingsport on the specially designed railroad car for the occasion. The railroad offered special round-trip fares for the day for people to ride the train with Santa and come to Kingsport to do their Christmas shopping. Santa requested that children along the Clinchfield Railroad that could not come to Kingsport be sure to be at their respective railroad stations so Santa could talk with them. The Santa Train is a tradition still very much alive today.

November 27, 1941

Thanksgiving Dinner

Thanksgiving dinner was held today at the City Mission. According to Thomas A. William, superintendent of the Kingsport City Mission, the dinner was to be for those who would otherwise not have the privilege of a "big" meal that day. Kingsporters were encouraged and invited to give food for the meal. Williams had been superintendent of the City Mission since it was founded in April 1936. The mission, located on Sullivan Street, operated as a nondenominational social service organization. After Thomas Williams died in 1967, his wife, Clara Williams, took over operations of the City Mission and continued to run it until its closing.

November 28, 1958

Santa Arrives

Santa Claus arrived today around 5:30 p.m. on the Santa Special Train. Arriving at the Clinchfield Railroad Station, Santa boarded a fire truck for a parade through the business district. Merchants from around the city accompanied Santa and passed out candy and gifts. For the occasion, Christmas decorations had been put up, and a Christmas tree was officially lit, signaling the official Christmas shopping season. Lights also went on the revolving Christmas tree in Church Circle.

November 29, 1925

Kingsport Men Bound on Murder Charge

Ira Linkous and Mart Hutson were bound over to circuit court without bond on a charge of robbing and murdering Jake Hensley after the preliminary hearing. The prosecution presented ten witnesses during the preliminary hearing, and circumstantial evidence against the two was strong. The defense only produced one witness, but the testimony failed to provide much weight for the defense. The body of Hensley was found on the highway under a railroad trestle. A bullet hole was found on the body, and his wallet was missing. Hensley was only about one hundred yards from his home when he was killed. The investigation into his death led to Linkous, Hutson and Kirk Jones. Jones was released during the first preliminary hearing.

November 30, 1916

Happenings of the Methodists of Kingsport

The *Johnson City Comet* announced that the Methodists of Kingsport expected to give a Sunday school Christmas Festival complete with a tree and program at the Methodist church on the Wednesday of Christmas week. Presents would be provided for any child that attended, and Santa Claus was expected to attend the festival. It also reported that the mystery supper given by the ladies of the church at the school building was a success. The supper was attended by a large crowd, and the funds raised went toward furnishing the church building. Lastly, it was reported that Reverend Wampler, pastor of Broad Street Methodist, would preach on Sunday morning at 11:00 a.m. at Old Kingsport Presbyterian Church.

DECEMBER

December 1, 1955

Woman Aided Jailbreak

Eugenia Dykes, a forty-five-year-old nurse, confessed to helping Ralph Cozzolino escape from jail. She admitted to providing Cozzolino with saw blades and driving him to Kingsport from Blountville on the night of the escape. Eight prisoners escaped with Cozzolino. Dykes met Cozzolino at Holston Valley Community Hospital, where she was employed and he was being treated for a broken ankle. The injury occurred during a getaway attempt after he robbed the Piggly Wiggly in Kingsport. After she was arrested, Dykes refused bond and spent the night in jail. Against her wishes, her husband posted bond the next day. Dykes was charged and convicted of aiding and abetting a felon to escape jail In July 1956, she was given a suspended sentence of eleven months and twenty-nine days. Attorney General Lacy West said the decision was made after a long and very heated deliberation but that Dykes had suffered enough.

December 2, 1926

Kingsport Movie

This day was the second and last day to catch a presentation of the successful local movie *Kingsport*. The movie was a local talent film being shown at the Strand Theatre. Filmed here in Kingsport by the Story-Art Pictures Corporation, the film featured an all-Kingsport cast picked from the local talent. The theme was woven into the movie using the local background of places around the city. The plot focused on Mr. and Mrs. Henpeck, played by Bob Snow and Ella Weatherby, and the "baby" played by Katherine Adair. Fred Mayhew played the city sheik, and Bobby Dodd played the part of the cub reporter for the daily newspaper. The movie featured a thrilling automobile chase through the business district of Kingsport.

December 3, 1964

Nick Showalter

Nick Showalter, Dobyns-Bennett High School quarterback, was selected to the second team United Press International's (UPI) All-State Football Squad. Last week, Showalter was placed on the first team Associated Press's (AP) squad; he had won numerous other awards and credits stemming from his football achievements. At Dobyns-Bennett, he was on a state championship team. Showalter went on to play football for the University of Tennessee Volunteers under Coach Doug Dickey. During his time at Tennessee, the Vols won the SEC and National Title in 1967 and played in three bowl games. In 1967, he was a second team All-SEC selection by the Associated Press at defensive end, proving that he was a capable offensive and defense player. Showalter stayed in Knoxville after college and became a prominent dentist often referred to as "Dr. Nick." Nick Showalter died in 2012.

December 4, 1967

Holston River Bridge

The Holston River Bridge collapsed under the weight of a thirteen-ton truck. The truck, driven by Clarence Kingen, was crossing the bridge on South Eastman Road about 4:25 p.m. when it gave way, dropping the span and the truck into the Holston River. He escaped with no injury. Kingen was en route from Waynesboro, Virginia, to Limestone, Tennessee, carrying a load of thirty cases of frozen food for the Oakwood Market in Colonial Heights. Kingen missed his turn on Highway 81 and was directed to Highway 23, Eastman Road. Kignen said he saw no warning signs as he approached the bridge, which had a five-ton limitation. The truck landed in the river tilted on its right side, but Kingmen was able to climb on top of the truck and was rescued by a Kingsport Lifesaving Crew boat. No charges were expected to be filed.

December 5, 1919

Coal Shortage

It was announced on this day that nearly all of Kingsport's industries might be suspending operations within the next few days because of the coal shortage. The Kingsport Brick Company had already closed its plant. The Clinchfield Portland Cement Company, the Kingsport Pulp Corporation, the Kingsport Extract Corporation and the Kingsport Tanneries faced suspension as soon as any work in progress currently was completed. Only the Kingsport Hosiery Mill would be allowed to continue, and only for forty-eight hours a week, since its power was generated by the Kingsport Utilities. The other plants, which normally operated on a continuous basis on their own energy, could not obtain coal. If the plants were suspended, nearly two thousand workmen would be out of work until the factories could obtain coal.

December 6, 1947

Circus Cabaret

The Kingsport Junior Auxiliary hosted a Circus Cabaret at the Civic Auditorium this evening. The event would provide entertainment for families and couples according to Mrs. H.J. Nance, president of the guild. There would be dancing, sideshows, games and refreshments. A highlight of the show was the golden dress parade. Stuart Allen of the Jerome H. Cargill Production Company of New York directed the show, with Frank Taylor as ringmaster. Mrs. W.S. Argabright served as the chairman of the program. Proceeds from the show were used to furnish and maintain a room at city hall for temporarily lodging juvenile delinquents.

December 7, 1943

"E" Award

On this day, Tennessee Eastman Company and Holston Ordnance Works were presented with the Army-Navy "E" Award. The Army-Navy "E" Award was an honor presented to companies during World War II for excellence in production of war equipment and contributions to the war

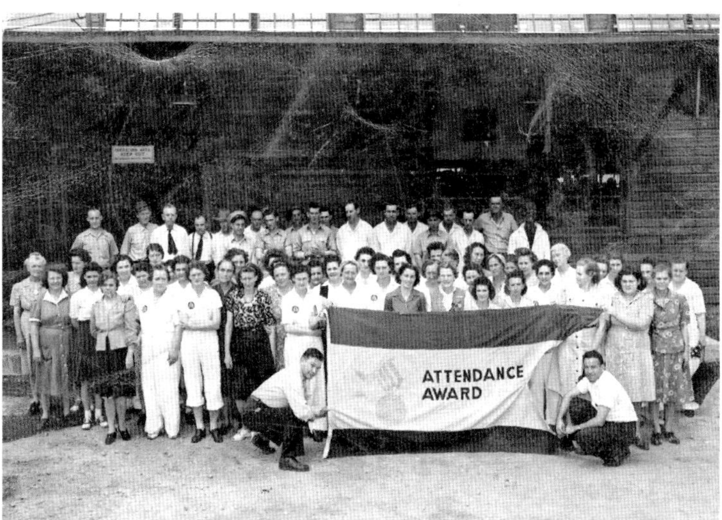

Holston Ordnance Works employees. *Archives of the City of Kingsport.*

effort. The award was also known as the Army-Navy Production Award. Holston Ordnance Works manufactured RDX, a powerful explosive, for the military during World War II. During this time, Holston Ordnance Works was managed by Tennessee Eastman Company. Construction of Holston Ordnance Works began in 1942, but it wasn't fully operational until mid-1943. Holston Ordnance Works became the largest maker of high explosives in the world. At its peak, Holston Ordnance Works employed close to seven thousand people. Forty percent of those employed were women.

December 8, 1949

Local Gang Comedy

A two-reel film dubbed a local gang comedy was showing at the State Theater. Filmed in Kingsport by Melton Barker Productions, all of the characters in the comedy were children from Kingsport. The film began with Betty Davis, the lead in the film, being kidnapped and carried off to a shack. Her sister, Jean, reported the kidnapping to the local gang. One little boy was too small to go on the hunt for Betty, so he organized a gang of his own. The stars in the film were Sandra Kay Wheeler, Pamela Ann O'Toole and Daniel Lee Ball. Around two hundred other local kids were also cast in the movie.

December 9, 1919

Community Hospital Buyout

Nine Kingsport physicians purchased the Community Hospital, formerly operated by the city: Dr. C.P. Edwards, Dr. E.W. Tipton, Dr. O.S. Hauk, Dr. P.E. Marsh, Dr. J.B. Millard, Dr. Lewis Highsmith, Dr. W.H. Reed, Dr. G.G. Keener, Dr. T.B. Yancey and Dr. Joseph Pinquard. Ruth Hampton of Chattanooga was hired as superintendent of the hospital. She replaced Dr. Edna Brown, who resigned the previous week to take up a course in anesthetics at Tulane Hospital. Dr. Edna Brown was the first female doctor in Kingsport.

December 10, 1923

Tobacco Warehouse Open

Kingsport's tobacco warehouse, which was introduced to the public on December 1 with a big tobacco rally, opened for sales on this day. The warehouse was located on Main and Island Streets and constructed for an estimated $25,000. The building was a large one-story structure with brick walls, cement floors and three driveways for unloading tobacco. Work on the warehouse started in August, and it was sold by the Kingsport Tobacco Market Inc. to the Burley Tobacco Grower's Cooperation Association. Tobacco farmers from across the region were encouraged to visit the warehouse. Only those with membership in the Burley Tobacco Grower's Cooperation Association were allowed to sell their tobacco through the warehouse.

December 11, 1923

Gemmel Brothers

The Gemmel Brothers officially opened to the buying public today in their new location on Market Street. The company was a local branch of the store in Bristol that carried the same name. The electrical company was outfitted with attractive displays in the building's large show windows. In the rear of the building there was a large stock room, and there were rooms for displays of fixtures and electrical supplies. According to J.A. Murray, the local manager of the store, the building that housed the new store was remodeled, the stock installed and displays set in only five working days.

December 12, 1937

Nu-Joy Beauty Shop

Clara Williams made an announcement today that she was working at the Nu-Joy Beauty Shop. Williams, former owner of Clara Beauty Shop, was one of Kingsport's first beauty operators and had worked in Kingsport for twelve years. The Nu-Joy Beauty Shop was located in the new Cherokee Building, on the corner of Cherokee and New Streets. The Cherokee Building stood across the street from Allen's Chevrolet Garage. Williams invited her many friends to visit her at the new shop. Parking for the beauty shop was available on New Street. Williams had been a resident of Kingsport since 1918 and was a co-founder of the City Mission.

December 13, 1936

Christmas Bonuses

Forty-six employees of Dobyns-Bennett Hardware Company, Kingsport Hardware Company and Elizabethton Hardware Company were guests of officials of the corporation at a banquet at the Kingsport Inn. A musical program led by Allen Dryden Sr. provided Christmas songs. Frank Taylor and his jug band were followed by a program of singing and dancing by students of Douglass High School. Following the dinner, G.W. Taylor, president of the company, made a brief talk in which he expressed his gratitude for the cooperation and efficiency of the employees of the company. Taylor continued by saying that the company planned to continue to share profits with its employees. At the end of the night, officials distributed Christmas checks to the employees totaling $1,200.

December 14, 1928

Kingsport General

The first operation at the new Kingsport General Hospital occurred on this day. The new hospital, formerly the Riverview Hospital, was located on Charlemont and then called the Kingsport General Hospital. The hospital building was converted from the Charlemont apartments and equipped to handle twenty-two patients. The hospital had reception rooms and operating rooms, and an addition to the hospital was planned for the spring. It would include room for an X-ray room and a laboratory. Until then, the X-ray facilities would continue to be housed at the offices of Drs. Reed and Tipton on Broad Street. The hospital was one of the best equipped in the area and open to outside doctors for operations at all times.

December 15, 1958

Cold Wave

Sunny skies would not warm up the Kingsport area after a four-and-one-half-inch snowfall. Fair and cold was the outlook for the day. The area's first measurable snow was part of a snowstorm that started through the South last week and moved northward up the Eastern Seaboard, dumping snow of various depths. This snow was the heaviest accumulation in Kingsport since February 1958, when six inches covered the city. Other than causing some road hazards, the weather had not made a huge impact or caused much damage in the Kingsport area. Intermountain Telephone Company and Kingsport Utilities reported there were no telephone or power interruptions. Dana F. Swick, superintendent of Kingsport City Schools, reported that there were no plans to close the schools.

December 16, 1950

Increase in Milk Prices

Effective today, the price of milk would be increased one cent per quart in Kingsport. All three diary companies—PET, Foremost and Southern Maid—announced they would all be raising their prices at the same time. The increase came from the rising costs of raw materials and operating expenses. Albert Lowe, manager of PET Dairy Company, noted that producers of raw milk had seen increases in cost, necessitating the increase for consumers. Quarts of sweet milk were now twenty-two cents, pints eleven and a half.

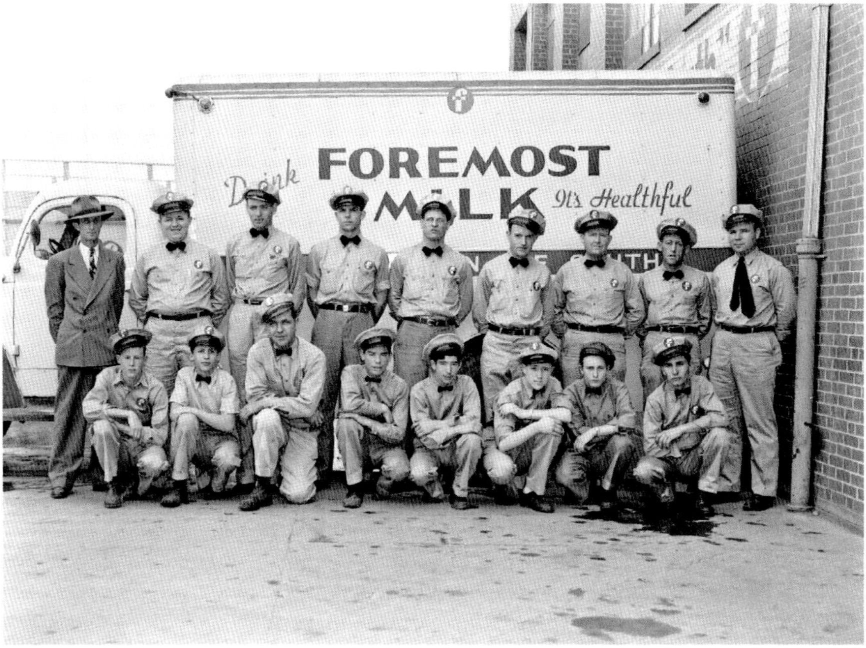

Employees of Foremost Dairies. *Archives of the City of Kingsport.*

December 17, 1931

J.A. Bagley Found Murdered

J.A. Bagley, thirty, of Tranbarger Hollow in the Lynn Garden section of Kingsport, was found shot to death. His body was found facedown in the road about two hundred yards from his car. Deputy Sheriff Thompson noted that from all general indications, Bagley was shot three times. The first while still in his car, the second after he exited the car and the third after he had fallen to the ground. Arthur Copas and Ray Lane were being held in connection with the crime, but the Kingsport Police Department declined to disclose the possible connection.

December 18, 1948

Kingsport Lifesaving Crew

The Kingsport Lifesaving Crew took its first call on this day in 1948 and has been responding to emergency calls since. The original Kingsport Lifesaving Crew consisted of fire chief C.M. Kenner, John Stiles, W.T. Bond, Clarence Rector, J.B. Weaver, W.A. Bryant Sr., Ralph Burke, Ralph Deal, T.E. Gavin, J.C. Perry and J.C. Jones. The group got its start when a group of civic leaders came together and discussed the need for an emergency rescue organization. They reached out to Julian Wise, "Mr. Rescue Squad," in Virginia for assistance in starting an organization. The Kingsport Lifesaving Crew later became the Kingsport Lifesaving and First Aid Crew Inc. The fire on Market Street in 1949, in which fireman Ray Hicks lost his life, was the first big disaster that the lifesaving crew worked on. Arriving minutes after the fire department, they were able to provide oxygen masks.

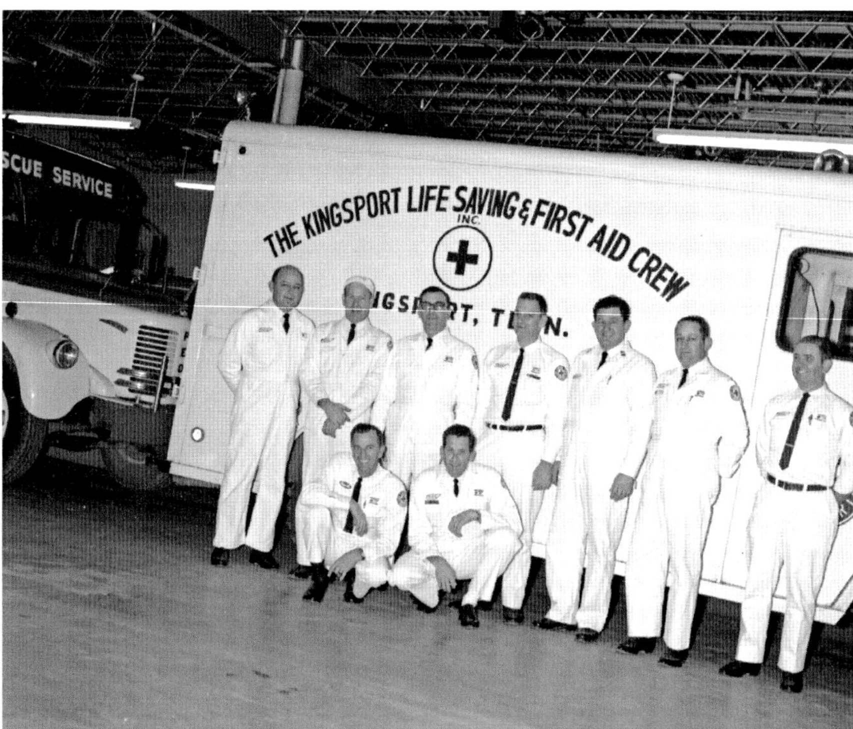

Kingsport Lifesaving and First Aid Crew. *Archives of the City of Kingsport.*

December 19, 2011

YMCA and Kingsport Aquatic Center

The City of Kingsport and the Greater Kingsport Family YMCA broke ground on the Kingsport Aquatic Center and the adjoining YMCA Wellmont Center in the MeadowView area on this day. The project would serve the Kingsport area by offering aquatic events, lessons and leisure opportunities to citizens and visitors while also expanding the Y's ability to positively affect the everyday lives of children, adults and families. The Kingsport Aquatic Center's outdoor water park, featuring a large pool with a water playground and lily pad crossing, two water slides, a nine-hundred-foot lazy river and a concession area, held its grand opening in May 2013.

December 20, 1941

Baylor-Nelms Fire

Early on this morning, firefighters were still working on a fire at the Baylor-Nelms Furniture Company on Broad Street. The fire originated in the basement and significantly damaged the first floor, including furniture, electrical appliances and other merchandise. The fire department reported that the fire damage in the building would be high but that damage from smoke and water would be the worst of it. The business was located in three adjoining store buildings. The fire started in the basement of 125 Broad Street, and when the firemen arrived, the three-story building was full of smoke, and masks had to be worn to get into the building.

December 21, 1931

Orgie Cox Killed

William Orgie Cox of Highland Park was stabbed to death during a drunken brawl inside Poston's store around 8:30 p.m. Cox died as a result of a wound made with a blade of more than thirteen inches. It is believed the knife severed a vital organ. Alden Doty and Jess Simpson were being held on first-degree murder charges. Doty and Simpson were sentenced to eighteen years in the penitentiary, but the men were granted new trials. While awaiting a new trial, Doty escaped from prison. Upon his capture, he faced additional charges for his jailbreak. Simpson was later exonerated of the charges while Doty was given a two- to ten-year prison sentence.

December 22, 1945

Strand Theatre Burns Down

Thousands of Christmas shoppers lined the streets of Downtown Kingsport to watch as firefighters battled the raging fire at the Strand Theatre. The Strand Theatre was destroyed, and the fire threatened to damage the J. Fred Johnson and Company building next door. Nearly eight hundred moviegoers, a packed house, were in the Strand when the fire started. Luckily, alert theater employees were able to safely evacuate the building. At one time, all four of the city's fire trucks were in use, and all but one firefighter was at the scene. One truck and ten men from the Holston Ordnance Works joined in the efforts to control the fire. Firefighters from Johnson City were also called to the scene. It was believed the theater building was a total loss. The Strand was rebuilt after the fire and reopened in 1947.

December 23, 1940

Tommy McNeer Injured in Crash

Thomas "Tommy" McNeer Jr., photographer and son of Dr. and Mrs. T.T. McNeer, was injured in an automobile accident near Fort Myers, Florida. McNeer was with the Kingsport High School basketball team on its tour through Florida and Cuba when the accident occurred. McNeer was driving his Chevrolet coupe in the rain when the car struck a soft shoulder and became uncontrollable. The car plunged down an embankment, injuring McNeer in the process. He was the only one in the car at the time of the accident. Dr. and Mrs. McNeer were on their way to Miami, Florida,

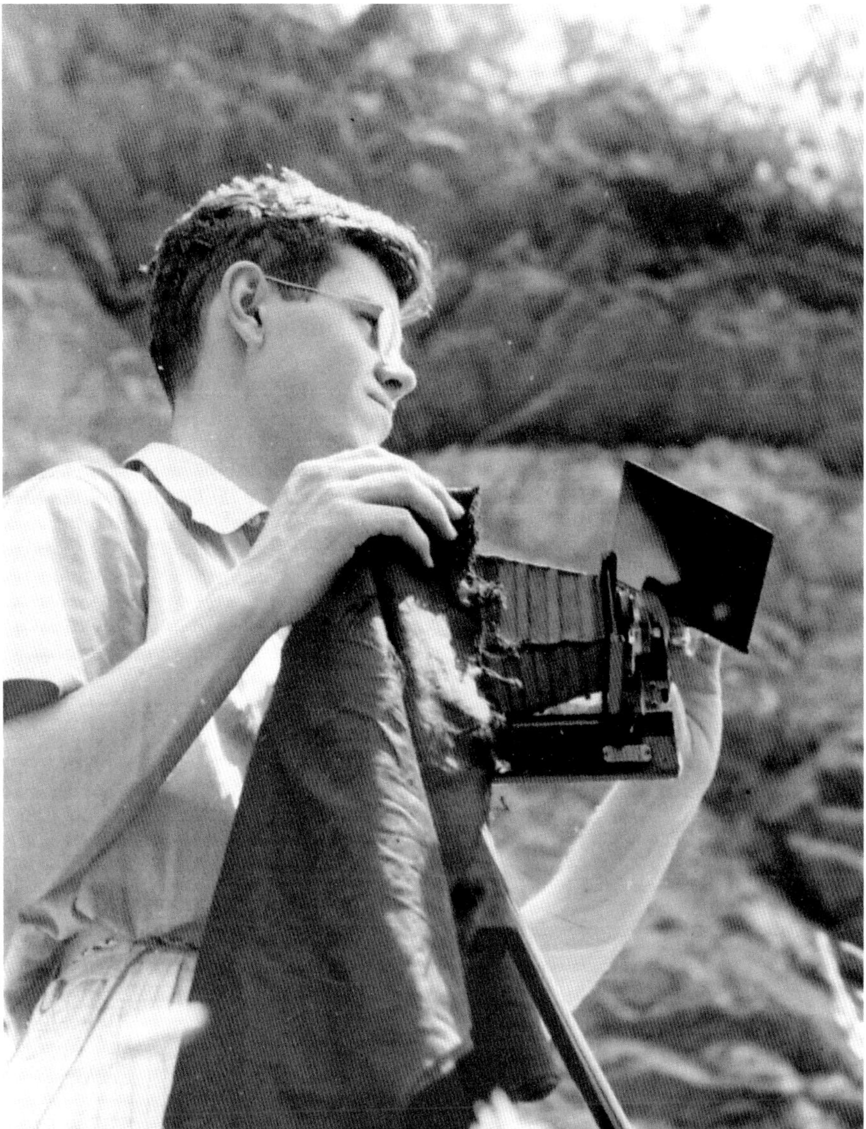

Thomas McNeer Jr. with camera. *Archives of the City of Kingsport.*

to see their son. Thomas McNeer Jr. had a successful career as a professional photographer in Kingsport for many decades.

December 24, 1956

Salvation Army Christmas Fund

The Salvation Army Christmas Fund reached a total of $2,748. Donations were boosted the previous week by the Christmas kettles and contributions made by individuals and groups. The employees of the Holston Defense Corporation canceled their annual Christmas party and donated the funds they normally would have spent to the Salvation Army. Members of the fire prevention department of the Holston Defense Corporation and the Holston Ordnance Works together made a collective contribution. With these and a special contribution from employees of shift number two of the Tenite Shipping Department at Tennessee Eastman Company, the Salvation Army provided free baskets of Christmas food for families in need.

December 25, 1940

DBHS Basketball Bound for Havana, Cuba

The annual tour of the Dobyns-Bennett High School basketball team through Florida and Cuba was regarded as one of the most unusual athletic stunts in the nation. LeRoy Sprankle and his team had spent the last ten years traveling to Florida and playing some of the best teams in the state. For the past two years, Havana, Cuba, had been included in that trip. On Christmas Day 1940, the team boarded a boat bound for Havana. These trips, taken during the Christmas break, became one of the major phases of life on the basketball team. Each year, the race to the varsity team, and the ensurance of going on the trip, had gotten tougher. Not only did the team play from six to ten games but the coaches also planned plenty of recreation and sightseeing along the way.

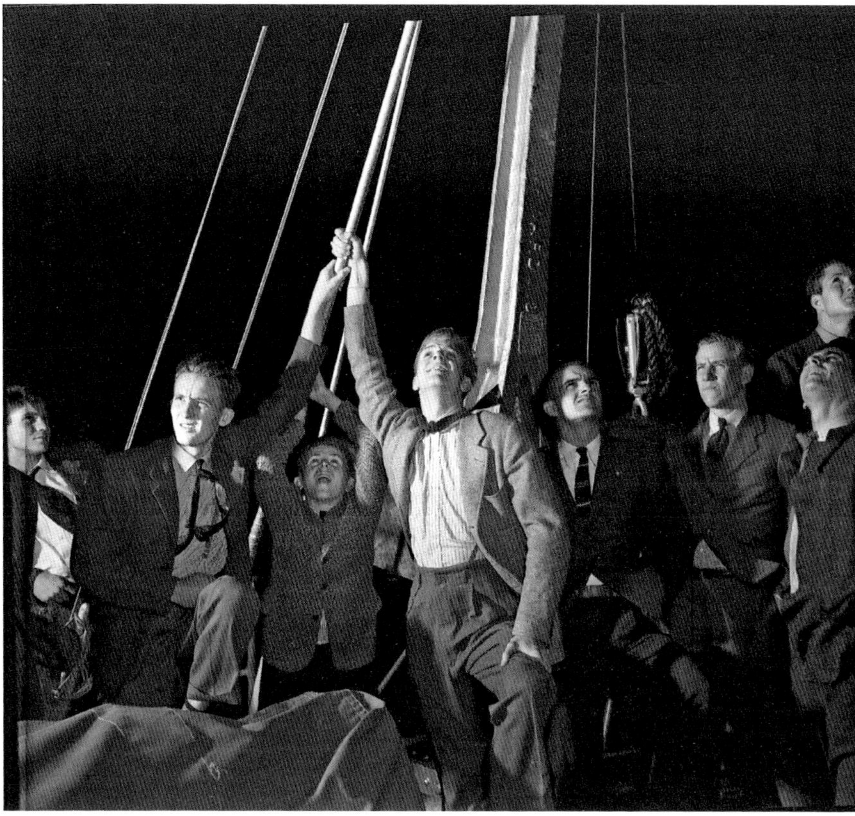

Dobyns-Bennett High School basketball team on a boat bound for Havana, Cuba. *Archives of the City of Kingsport.*

December 26, 1946

Informal Tea

Mrs. H.J. Shivell, her daughter Jane Stewart Shivell and Mrs. B.M. Brown hosted an informal tea at the Shivell home on Orchard Court this afternoon in honor of Miss Charlene Gay Edwards. Edwards, the daughter of Mr. and Mrs. C.P. Edwards Jr., would be getting married on December 30. More than sixty guests came to call on Edwards. Mrs. C.P. Edwards Jr. and Mrs. E.J. Nance presided over the tea table and punchbowl. Edwards wore a brown crepe, sequined-trimmed afternoon dress.

DECEMBER 27, 1964

Minister Shot

The Reverend Garland Clark, pastor of Long Island Primitive Church, was shot down in the street in front of the home of Willie Evans. Evans was the grandfather of Sam Riner, the seventeen-year-old boy who had been fatally stabbed a few months earlier. Jerry Clark, the reverend's son, had been charged in the death of Riner and charged with attempted murder for pushing Riner's younger brother into the Holston River. Clark was acquitted of all charges. The Reverend Clark was shot by Ronnie Eugene Riner, the sixteen-year-old brother of the slain Riner. The shooting occurred after a disagreement escalated. Reverend Clark was shot in the arm, and the bullet entered his stomach. He was at Holston Valley Community Hospital recovering, but Riner faced a charge of felonious assault with intent to commit murder and carrying arms.

DECEMBER 28, 1945

Actress Merle Oberon in Kingsport

One of Hollywood's brightest starts, Merle Oberon, was in Kingsport with her husband, Lucien Ballard. The two strolled down Broad Street and had dinner at the Kingsport Inn. They were in town for the night on a stop en route to Los Angeles. Traveling by car, they made Kingsport an overnight spot after hearing that it was an attractive and interesting city. NBC war correspondent Robert St. John and film star Bette Davis had recently visited Kingsport as well. Merle Oberon, born Estelle Merle O'Brien Thompson, was born in India, where she lived until the age of seventeen, when she left for London. She began her career in British films, came to the United States around 1934 and became a star in Hollywood. Her last film was *Interval*, in 1973. She died in 1979.

December 29, 1950

Miss Mary Ann Conant

Miss Mary Ann Conant and Mrs. Reed Altom represented the State of Tennessee in Washington, D.C., at a White House Mid-Century Conference on children and youth. The women gave a report on the conference on this day at 7:30 p.m. in the courthouse. Altom went to Washington, D.C., with Conant, a freshman at the University of Tennessee. Conant was chosen because of her outstanding work in 4-H.

December 30, 1936

Death of George L. Carter

George L. Carter, vice-president of the Carter Coal Company, passed away on this day in 1936. Carter, one of the greatest industrial developers and leaders in southern Appalachian coal, was stricken with pneumonia and passed away in a Washington, D.C. hospital. Carter was born on January 10, 1857, near the town of Hillsville in Carroll County, Virginia. Carter can be considered the founder of modern Kingsport. He was a visionary who realized the possibility of Kingsport and was responsible for bringing the Clinchfield Railroad to the area. It was his land acquisitions that led to the building of Kingsport. It was through his relationship with Carter that J. Fred Johnson came to Kingsport. Johnson, a longtime associate and brother-in-law of Carter's, helped coordinate the purchase of Carter's land from John B. Dennis, financier with Blair and Company of New York. Carter was survived by his widow, Mayetta Wilkinson, and one son, James Walter Carter.

December 31, 1929

Youth Killed in Accident

Kingsport youth Ronald Hicks, twelve, was killed in a hunting accident near Morison Chapel. Hicks, stepson of James Franklin Richards, an employee of the Tennessee Eastman Corporation, was hunting with Homer Ray and Frank Strong. Hicks was killed when Strong discharged a bullet into his head. Strong and Ray were arrested and held in the city jail. After a careful investigation, an inquest hearing determined the shooting to be an accident. This marked the second tragedy for Richards. His wife and two children, Laura Jeanette, six, and James Franklin Jr., three, were killed in a fire at their home near Borden Mill in 1927. Richards, who was at work at the time, was the only surviving member of the family.

SELECTED BIBLIOGRAPHY

Books

Egan, Martha Avaleen, and Nellie McNeil. *Kingsport*. Charleston, SC: Arcadia Publishing, 1998.

Kingsport: City of Industries, Schools, Churches and Homes. Kingsport, TN: Rotary Club, 1937.

Long, Howard. *Kingsport: A Romance of Industry*. Kingsport, TN: Sevier Press, 1928.

Stahl, Ray, and Ned Irwin. *The Last Empire Builder: A Life of George L. Carter, 1857–1936*. Johnson City: East Tennessee State University Press, 2012.

Wolfe, Margaret Ripley. *Kingsport, Tennessee: A Planned American City*. Lexington: University Press of Kentucky, 1987.

Wright, Brianne. *Downtown Kingsport*. Charleston, SC: Arcadia Publishing, 2011.

Newspapers

Johnson City Comet
Kingsport Mirror
Kingsport News
Kingsport Post
Kingsport Times
Kingsport Times-News

ABOUT THE AUTHOR

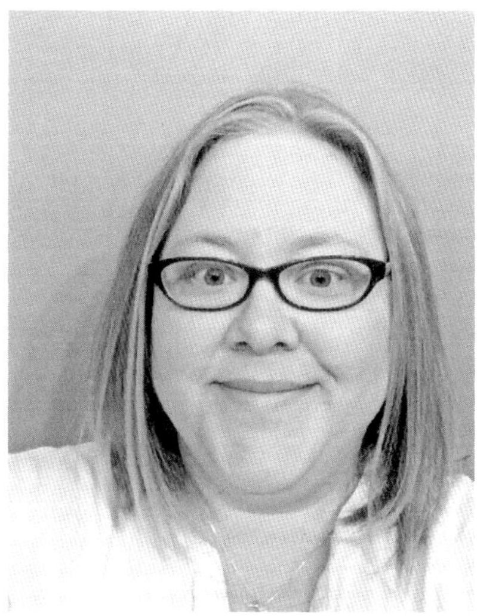

Brianne Wright has been the archivist for the city of Kingsport since 2007. She is the author of Images of America: *Downtown Kingsport* (Arcadia Publishing, 2011). She graduated from the University of Tennessee and received her master's degree in archival studies from East Tennessee State University. She was a recipient of the East Tennessee Historical Society's Award of Excellence in 2014. She lives in Church Hill, Tennessee, with her husband, Mitch, and daughter, Lily.